We're All Zombies Now

Revised and Expanded

Additional tools for parents and people looking for ways to keep themselves and their children away from Porn.

Biz Gainey

Copyright © 2018 Biz Gainey

All rights reserved.

ISBN: 9780692875643

DEDICATION

I dedicate this book to my wife, for loving me in the midst of and through my addiction.

To my children, for patiently believing and hoping that my addiction would not win.

To my church family, for their redemptive hand in my healing which gave me the courage to share my story.

To my community, which is soon to face the Porn-Tsunami yet to come.

CONTENTS

	Acknowledgments	i
1	**A PERSONAL JOURNEY:** *Addiction, Freedom, and the Power of Hope in a Good and Beautiful God*	1
2	**PORNOGRAPHY'S PATTERNS OF DEHUMANIZATION:** *Exploring and Identifying Porn's Patterns of Destruction and Dehumanization*	Pg 9
3	**POWER OF THE GOSPEL:** *The Power of the Gospel and the Joy of living a Porn-Free Life*	Pg 25
4	**RECOGNIZING AND RESPONDING TO YOUR UNIQUE TRAPS AND TRIGGERS:** *LEARNING HOW TO AVOID TEASING SENSATION, TEMPTING SITUATION, AND THE TRAP-DAY*	Pg 32
5	**DEVELOPING FAMILY PROTOCOLS AND PREVENTION:** *PROTECTING YOUR CHILDREN FROM PORN*	Pg 48
6	**PRACTICING RHYTHMS OF GRACE:** *Experiential Practices as a Reliable Pathway Toward Freedom*	Pg 67
7	**PILLARS OF PERSONAL FREEDOM:** *Discovering Four Repeatable Pillars of Freedom and Restoration*	Pg 84
8	**Pathways to Freedom Within Community:** *Enjoy Discover an Ongoing Process of Freedom*	Pg 88
9	**Rebuilding and Restoring:** *Re-Ordering a Life that Has Been Ravaged by Porn*	Pg 94
10	**A Forty Day Journey Into Freedom From Addiction:** *An Invitation to an Ongoing and Ever-Changing Journey of Denial and Delight (focusing on technology)*	Pg 108

ACKNOWLEDGMENTS

I'd like to express my gratitude to the many people who stories of faith and fortitude help make this book possible! To those who helped me editing this book, Julie Palmer and Theresa Hennis, your participation and skillful eyes have only made this book better. For any errors the reader encounters here, they are of my own making. To my wife, whose gentle hand and loving conviction toward truth in all things has helped me believe in myself more than I dared to hope. To the many friends and family members who walked with me and guided me along the way: Denny Huebner, Mark Shaner, Elton Hume, Ed Bamberg, Roger Feeback, Greg Wiens, Barry Haslett, Tim Smick, the debt of gratitude I owe to you (and many more) would require a thousand lifetimes to repay! To Dan Nafe, who once said, "Hey, this stuff might make a pretty good read," I give my thanks!

To my children, Jacob, Luke and Hayla, the life you are yet to live makes this effort, meager as it is, all the more rewarding. My hope is that you will inherit a world that's free of porn and its dehumanizing power.

To my Lord and His Gospel I give my fullest thanks! It's the Gospel of grace to which I have run again and again, to find gracious reception, a gentle but firm invitation to repentance and the extravagant gift of restoration-hope.

1 A PERSONAL JOURNEY

ADDICTION, FREEDOM, AND THE POWER OF HOPE IN A GOOD AND BEAUTIFUL GOD!

More than three decades ago I stumbled into pornography while spending the night with a friend. I was twelve. In those days (the early eighties), a kid had to go to extraordinary measures to obtain and consume porn. Once I consumed, I was hooked. It only took one image, ripped from a "girly" magazine, to reel me in! I would remain hooked – addicted – to porn for the next 16 years. By the time I faced – truly faced - my addiction and recognized it as such, I was twenty-eight-years old. I was married, in ministry, and expecting my first child. Everything in my life was beautiful except for the reality that porn had captured my heart and was secretly consuming my soul.

Whatever captures your heart controls your behavior. *Once Upon a Time*, a television program my wife and I watch, animates this truth on a regular basis. The early seasons of the show feature an "evil queen" who reaches inside one's chest and literally extracts their heart. When the queen has your heart, she has you in her control. It always leads to destruction, and it often leads to death.

Though it took a while for my addiction to be exposed, eventually it was. One night my wife caught me viewing porn. She walked in on me watching porn through the local cable programming (yeah, the dark ages). Consumed, I failed to hear her footsteps as she entered the room. Though I tried to switch the channel, it was too late. She had seen enough. She was heartbroken and humiliated. For the first time, I began to clearly see the power my addiction had over me and the pain it caused those around me!

I remember the moment as if it were yesterday. Caught in a self-inflicted porn consumption prison, I heard her voice say, "Everything about you is beautiful. And then there is this **filth**." I reached for her. She cringed. I tried to speak, to tell her how sorry I was. She glared. At that moment, my very presence was revolting; my touch was nauseating.

The moment my wife caught me was the absolute low point of my marriage. Looking back on that moment, over twenty years later, I see that it was also the beginning of a long, protracted, courageous, and harrowing journey into freedom.

Around the age of twenty eight, I began my *heart reclamation* journey.

In order to move forward on my journey I soon learned that I needed a complete "re-orientation." By the time I decided to face the problem, I had been involved in consistent porn consumption for nearly sixteen years.

In those days (the late 1990s) getting help was not so easy. There were, to my knowledge, very few tools or resources that helped one break free of porn's grip. However, with the aid of my wife, a trusted friend, and a counselor, I began my slow walk out of porn. It's a walk that continues to this day. My walk has been one of many ups and downs.

There have been moments of deep sadness and mountains of great joy. There have been times when the grip of porn was so tight it felt as though I would collapse in loss of breath. There have been other moments when I have not felt the slightest of temptations to consume porn – long seasons of wonder and joy. I am not equipped to tell you why I still experience both of these realities, even down to this day.

But I can pass along a truth that I cling to daily*:*

There is no time like the present moment to free yourself from your porn addiction and recapture your heart.

This has become my personal 'rally cry." Yes. Out of the ashes, beauty has formed. Take heart. As one trapped - for nearly two decades - in a relentless cycle of porn addiction, I want you to know that you can be free. Your life, marriage, home, work, family, etc., can flourish.

Porn addiction doesn't have to be the last word or the defining reality of your life! I am now (at the time of this writing) forty-six-years old. My wife and I are flourishing. We have three wonderful teen-aged children. I experience freedom from my addiction on a daily basis. I have for some time! It is possible for you, too! I am not perfect. I still struggle, and I continue to bear the marks and scars of the bruises, bumps, and breaks from previous failures.

Some years ago I attended the initial Gathering of the Apprentice Institute's Journey in Discipleship
(http://apprenticeinstitute.org/apprentice-experience/).

The Institute requires a trip to Kansas, which keeps me away from home for six days. Three days before I departed, my wife, Melissa, flew to Arkansas with our boys to visit a college campus. I would be away from Melissa for *nine* days. Two decades of porn consumption changes one's orientation entirely: to God, themselves, others, and the world around them. When you view porn long enough, *everyone and everything is porned*, to one degree or another. People, places, and passions become tools and objects, *means to be leveraged* in one's perpetual need to satisfy the cravings and urges, which are simmering deep within.[i]

Therefore, such an extended time away from Melissa – a couple of decades ago – would have been an absolute disaster. Trips like this are ready-made for porn's destructive allure. For many years now, such trips have not led me down the pathway to porn's fleeting pleasure. I am finding – wonderfully so – that my hunger for Melissa's embrace only grows. This experience of freedom was palpable during this particular week away–instilling confidence and absorbing hope. This experience has caused me to reflect on an important question:

> *Why am I finally - at this stage of life's journey - experiencing true freedom and enjoying the hope of lasting change, and how did I get here?*

An easy – and expected answer – might be that I was, on this particular occasion, on a spiritual retreat designed to nurture my faith and renew my soul. During past retreats – when I struggled in porn's pulsating grip – I did not experience the freedom I now enjoy. In fact, I remember the hard work and rigor required to stay clean and resist temptation during those long, and often exhausting, trips away from home (more on that to come).

Unfortunately, statistical data shows that far too many pastors are trapped in porn's grip, and even more parishioners are trapped in the addiction and *shame-sworn* to its secrecy.[ii]

Being on a spiritual retreat provides no safeguard: for some, sadly, it's simply an opportunity.

I discovered – while at the Apprentice Institute Gathering – that the false narratives which drew me to porn's pulsating grip have – over time – been scrubbed out of my heart and mind by the force of true narratives which draw me toward the good, loving, and lasting embrace of God. I use the term narrative to mean stories that captivate our hearts and minds.

Narratives are the stories that help us navigate our world. The stories that captivate us, shape our behavior, and determine our orientation to the world. The stories and narratives that captivate us develop over time and through experience.

James Smith, in <u>A Good and Beautiful God: Falling in Love with the God Jesus Knows,</u>[iii] suggests three dominant narratives that shape our orientation to and behavior in the world around us.

1. **Family Narratives**. These are the stories we learn from our biological family or the family environment in which we were raised. These stories shape the answer to life's most elemental questions:

    Why am I here?

Who am I?
Am I good enough, smart enough, pretty enough, etc.?

Will I be loved?

What must I do to be loved?

2. **Cultural Narratives.** These stories are derived from the images the culture around us finds valuable and reinforces through the institutions that sustain it. The images within our culture shape the stories in our heads that lead us to orient ourselves in a certain way toward the larger culture and people around us.

3. **Religious Narratives.** These are typically a combination of the first two with the added benefit of the images that dominate wider religious/church culture during one's lifetime. They are learned by way of hearing sermons, reading books, attending Sunday School, Vacation Bible School, etc.

The premise of this book is that we all live *by, through, and into story*. Our task is to identify the narrative or story by which we live and discover whether it's true or false. Here's the deal: false narratives – regardless of their point of origin – lead us to false loves and ultimately distort our desires and realign our hearts. True narratives lead us to true loves that align our heart with God and His loving embrace.

FALSE NARRATIVES THAT DROVE ME TOWARD THE PULL OF PORN

Confession as I begin: my false narratives are not easy to share. I debated whether or not I should share them. Melissa – as always – is a great encouragement to me. She believes that sharing these in a personal and candid way may help others experience true freedom and lasting change. Though these false narratives have been replaced, there was a time when I listened to them.

I have confessed these fully before Christ and received the warming embrace of his white-hot forgiveness and the full joy of His love. To recall them reminds me how terribly destructive they were and may be to others today.

Some false narratives that plagued me and led me toward Porn's distorted pleasure:

1. **YOU ARE NOT ENOUGH.** This initial false narrative is the one which birthed the others. Its power is found in the reality that it attacks and sabotages person-hood. Such lies are distortions and inversions of the truth grounded in Creation. Such lies left me open and vulnerable to the power of addiction, which manifested itself in pornography at a very early age.

2. **YOUR LIFE IS NOT ENOUGH.** This is a natural extension of the previous narrative. If "I" am not enough, then surely the life I live, the people around me, the experiences I have, etc., will never be enough.

3. **IF PEOPLE KNEW WHO YOU REALLY ARE THEY WOULD 'WRITE YOU OFF' AS A FRIEND.** This third narrative is, eventually, where I landed after believing the first two. The ultimate assault in each of these narratives is against what I consider Signature Affections. These Affections, on which I elaborate later, are the creational and sacred gifts of *person-hood, plac'dness and purpose* – each of which, I believe, is close to the heart of God.

A full-bodied, interior sense of personhood, plac'dness, and purpose (each of which is God-given) minimizes our proclivity to practice destructive behaviors and prevents us from developing habitual, pervasive, and life-extracting addictions.

Porn leverages false narratives in moments of weakness and loneliness to tempt us to taste her pleasures. Moments, I might add, that we all face. In those moments, porn – ever cloaked in secrecy and shame – draws us in. Porn's message attempts to fill that *inner longing and desire* by whispering promises that NEVER materialize.

The voice of porn, in these moments, might sound something like this:

1. **Take a minute and relax. Click this website.** I promise you will feel like you are enough when you see the women/men on this site ready to please you in every way possible.

2. **You deserve this.** After all, your wife will not do this for you. No, she will never be enough. Just join my chat room and let me give you what she never will.

3. **Everyone is doing this.** What harm could there possibly be in just a little click?

The *third voice* is, I believe, the most toxic of them all and seems to be the pervasive clamor in our culture today. There are, in other words, many people who see no harm in viewing porn, and their ranks appear to be growing! These people are – either through ignorance or arrogance – fools of the highest order. Do the research: when you do you will find statistical data indicating that porn addiction is the fuel that fires the engine of the global sex trade. *You will also find that the third largest criminal industry in the world is the buying and selling of women.* [iv] Yes, women – many who are as young as fourteen years old.

Porn's false narratives are as personal and powerful as they are global and pervasive. If you have been viewing porn for some time, then these narratives have both grown in number and strengthened their grip.

You cannot simply tell yourself that you aren't going to click anymore.

You can't just stop.

Maybe for an hour or two.

Maybe for a day or two. Maybe for a week or two.

There will come a time, however, in which you are tired, weary, lonely, and frustrated, and the false narrative's musical loop will begin playing its tune in your head.

If you don't replace false narratives with true (power) narratives, then you will be sucked in again.

Why?

Because pornography highjacks one's desire and pleasure pathways by leveraging false narratives that shape behavior. As such, consuming porn, over time, creates a whole set of neurological pathways that feed the addiction. As this happens, the false narratives reinforce porn's power by habituating the addict to 'act out' when certain triggers fire. Over time the porn addict has not simply established new patterns of behavior. She/he is literally enslaved by them and tethered to them.

Before I continue my story – which is one of freedom from pornography – I'd like to invite you into the future we're soon to inherit if we don't stem the tide of porn's destruction. It's a future that looks somewhat like the hit TV series *The Walking Dead*.

2 PORNOGRAPHY'S PATTERNS OF DEHUMANIZATION

EXPLORING AND IDENTIFYING PORN'S PATTERNS OF DESTRUCTION AND DEHUMANIZATION.

The Urban Dictionary defines Zombie Apocalypse as *"The end of the world by way of biochemically-regenerated humans whose only plan is to kill off all life on the planet.*

The entry goes on to add, somewhat melodramatically, **"Zombie Apocalypse has started; we must get to a safe place."**

Before I proceed, let me say – clearly – that I do not subscribe to the wildly popular notion of a *Zombie Apocalypse*. I am, however, intrigued by it and the media frenzy that has spawned from it.

One of the most popular series in 2015, in multiple categories, was The Walking Dead on AMC.[v] Zombie films, always a popular American movie genre, have grown exponentially in the past decade.[vi]

While I am by no means an expert on the Gothic or Zombie genre, I've discovered some characteristics that most Zombie movies and shows have in common.

They are:

1. Diminished or absent cognitive functioning.
2. Slumber pace of life – the sleep-walking or Zombie effect.
3. Mimicking the traits of rabid animals – insanity, aggressiveness, unwillingness, or inability to stop or cease their behavior.
4. Oblivious to other zombies and 'numb' to all but their appetite.
5. Insatiable need to consume flesh.
6. Cessation of normal biological requirements.

While there are many more that an expert eye would identify, these are several that I've seen again and again. The more I compare the common characteristics of a zombie story with the normative practices of modern society, I confess, there seems to be a zombie-esque quality to our culture.

Indeed, what I call the *dehumanization of humanity* is in the full bloom of spring, rather than the decomposition of winter. Even now, there are seasons in modern life where it's as if we are caught up in an unending episode of the hit TV series, *The Walking Dead*.

For example, there are few areas of cultural space where the **common good** finds welcome. Typically, we are a culture increasingly self-absorbed, quick to conflict, secure in strife, and content with our lack of communal qualities and abundance of individual rights.

While there are a multitude of reasons for this, I am going to propose *Three (highly personal and confessedly subjective) Reasons Pornography is Making Zombies of us All!*

Number 1: Porn Consumption Fosters Fantasy and Supplants Reality.

Years ago, while in seminary, I took a class on youth culture and contemporary trends. My professor, Dean Borgman, was fond of saying, "*If we don't encourage our youth to dream, they will become victims of fantasy.*" We are experiencing this reality today in unprecedented ways. Young people are consumed with fantasy and, as such, are becoming more and more disengaged with the world around them.

When I say fantasy I'm not referring to the classic genre, but with the experience of technology at the tip of our fingers – technology that both encourages and allows one to create and sustain a partial life based on partial truth. Pornography, as an industry, both leverages and exploits this current cultural reality to porn's favor and to our demise. In other words, the absence of dreams can create a vacuum that readily sucks one into a fantasy world of porn consumption.

Porn offers immediate gratification. We are served, gratified, and *purred over* in ways that provide a powerful but false sense of satisfaction. As the gratification received from porn falsifies reality it also supplants reality. Those of us who have ever struggled with this addiction know all too well how porn consumption contributes to and fosters a *non-participative* relationship with the world around us.

It does so by creating a false reality in which *we who consume are the center of attention and affection.*

Have you ever been around people who are *presently absent*? People who are always with you and somewhere else, simultaneously? Never engaged – fully detached? Such behavior *may* be a tale-tell sign of porn-consumption and addiction. Once rhythms of addiction become normative, the addiction's power lingers long after the moment of consumption occurs.

These rhythms of addiction then begin to influence and alter all other moments, all other situations, all other circumstances, all other relationships. Soon one becomes *presently absent* to all but the fantasy world which has been nurtured by the seductive song porn has sung.

In saying "porn consumption supplants reality," one might wonder if supplant is too strong a word. The physiological changes resulting from porn consumption are well attested. Our brains create neural pathways (or ruts) in which our experience with fantasy becomes normative and desirable.[vii]

Consider the following questions to help you determine the degree to which you, or someone you love, might be living this presently absent existence fueled by the rhythms of porn consumption/addiction:

Are you always and ever presently-absent to all but your inner fantasy and interior turmoil? In other words, is your fantasy always lurking just beneath the chaos of the moment?

Have you conveniently employed the "it's my personality" or the "it's how I'm wired" response when confronted?

Are your responses to otherwise normal inconveniences more extreme than normal? Are you often overreacting?

Are you restless and/or lethargic in moments when you should be content and engaged?

Porn consumption contributes to and fosters relational detachment, which leads to a non-communal community. If you are always detached, then the environments of your world will be non-communal and disconnected. Whatever your profession may be, your inability to engage is shaping your environment. Your marriage, family, church, work, and neighborhood are all being influenced by your lack of engagement in a meaningful and faithful manner.

Thus, porn addiction becomes increasingly more challenging to overcome. In fact, the moment reality fails to measure up, fantasy sings her seductive, soul-stirring song. We dance to her tune, usually in the dark of the night. We seek her shelter at the click of a mouse or the press of a thumb. Rhythmically, almost robotically, we dance our way back to fantasy. Supplanting is all but complete.

What then? **A Day of Reckoning.**

Many of us have faced that moment. For others, it's yet to come. For all, it eventually arrives.

Consider these outcomes of porn with the characteristics of a

Zombie Apocalypse. A *Zombie Apocalypse* would be populated with a sub-human people group who are:

1. Disengaged, presently-absent, and mindless.
2. Savagely attacking or escaping all that is flesh.
3. Diminished ability to determine right from wrong.
4. Unending need to consume without regard for the consumed.

We are already experiencing much of this in our world today, yet we remain blind to this peril. We, who fracture, often fail to spy the fractured. Our voice remains silent. We are silent, I suppose, because of our participation in and denial of these fractures – these similarities – we share with the *walking dead*. Indeed, we are all zombies now.

Once porn supplants reality, the addiction then begins to contribute to the distortion of reality and fosters a life gripped by porn's destructive desires.

Number 2: Porn Consumption Contributes to and Fosters the Distortion of Desire!

I love Golden Oreo cookies. I know the exact number of cookies in both the regular package as well as the family-size (my favorite) package. I eat about one *sleeve* per sitting. I know they are bad for me. Worse yet, I enjoy them most when reclining after dinner, just before bed. Consuming them expresses utter and irrevocable contempt for my *need* to stay in shape.

I understand the implications of the Golden Oreo ingredients. I know I shouldn't, yet I indulge. My wife watches (often in awe) as I consume. Melissa is a kind, gentle soul. She doesn't utter a terse word, nor flash a contemptible look. She sits and waits.

Because she loves me, she cannot sit idly by as I eat my way into a new insurance exception. She knows that even I will have to return the family-size (more per sleeve) Oreo package to the safety of our pantry. So she holds off; she waits. Then stealthily, in the dark of night, she *storms the beach of my Golden Oreo stronghold* and gently pulls the packaging open, ever so slightly, hardly noticeable. Enough to expedite the *slow crawl of cookie staleness* - on its own, no match for my ferocious appetite and uncontrollable desire.

Her covert assault works well enough for a day or two. Then, like an addict of old (taking the long way home, passing by the all-too-familiar haunt), I find myself idly cruising by the local grocery store. After a few passes I bring my car cautiously to a stop and rush feverishly inside. Once inside, I find myself wandering aimlessly into the cookie aisle . . .

Why do I give such energy to the consumption of food that I know is not good for me? Because I am a creature of desire.

Desire is God-given.

To desire is to be human.

Seemingly, my furnace of desire never stops firing.

C.S. Lewis, in <u>Mere Christianity</u>,[viii] suggests that we are a people of deep and unending desire. He further states that our unending quest for satisfaction reveals a deeper and often confounding truth about what it means to be human, what it means to be whole!

"If I find in myself a desire which no experience in this world can satisfy, the most probable explanation is that I was made for another world. If none of my earthly pleasures satisfy it, that does not prove that the universe is a fraud. Probably earthly pleasures were never meant to satisfy it, but only to arouse it, to suggest the real thing."

In his wonderful book, <u>Against an Infinite Horizon</u>,[ix] Ron Rolheiser opens with this quote from Karl Rahner:

"In the torment of the insufficiency of everything attainable we eventually learn

that here, in this life, all symphonies remain unfinished."

A failure to comprehend the truth behind this quote is to risk a life lost to reckless wandering: an unending and exhausting quest for the next person, place, or possibility to satisfy the hunger in our soul. To understand this, however, is to be one who, at last, has come to realize that our **desires are**, as Rolheiser asserts, **overcharged** for this life.

Or, as J.R.R. Tolkien offered,

"We all long for Eden, and we are constantly glimpsing it: our whole nature...is still soaked with the sense of exile."

Our whole nature is soaked with desire unfulfilled. Modern and ancient writers, poets, and artists have captured this sense of unending longing: the reality that all of our loves are made for Ultimate love! They have also captured the sense of despair accompanied by those moments when we settle for lesser loves in our quest for Ultimate love. This thread of love longed for and lost seems to weave its way through the fabric of human history.

Indeed, we are *overcharged for this life*. The discovery that I am overcharged for this life, or, as I would say, "*that I am an ever-firing furnace of desire*" - has led to several *Aha!* moments:

Aha! ~ The presence of this *ever-firing furnace of desire* is evidence of God's image.

Aha! ~ The presence of this *ever-firing furnace of desire* foreshadows my desire for unending life *with* God!

Aha! ~ The presence of this *ever-firing furnace of desire* singes others when I look to them to satisfy a desire which is satiated by God alone.

Aha! ~ The presence of this *ever-firing furnace of desire* burns me when I turn inward on my emptiness and seek to satiate my hunger through harmful addictions and 'isms' (work-a-holism, alcoholism, etc.).

Ah, yes! We desire, deeply so. The human journey, it might be said, is an unending and irrepressible desire to love and be loved. This desire is, however, easily distorted and misdirected (e.g., Golden Oreo Cookies over Golden Delicious Apples).

The porn industry taps into and exploits our fundamental desire and longing for intimacy.

If porn can tap into desire, it will distort desire.

Once desire is distorted, we then begin to behave in less fully human ways, *as if we are but shadows of our true selves.* Distorted desire disrupts the deeply meaningful moments and relationships of our lives. For example, when consuming porn, one might find it more enticing to sit alone, to escape to a room with a screen. Rather than resting in the company of those we love, porn rushes us toward a moment to sit alone, distorting our desires in the darkness of a fantasy.

In the moment of *sitting alone*, if one then consumes porn, an all-consuming loneliness creeps into the soul, taking up residence. Loneliness lingers and feelings of disconnection and detachment, when we are in the presence of others, begin to grow.

Eventually, participating in community requires too much of us and provides too little for us. Trapped inside ourselves, we fixate on images in our heads, offering delight, delivering distortion.

An apparent outcome of distorted desire - discernible in nearly every sector of our culture - is how we view or *image* others: **Porn consumption distorts one's image of others.**

Porn provides a disembodied experience (by which we disembody others) and feeds upon the images we are consuming. As we disembody others, we are disembodied.

We begin to relate to others from a *porn-fueled perspective*. We imagine others as instruments to be wielded for our pleasure, rather than persons of immense worth and sacred dignity.

Here is an experiment for you to consider: Find a space in your local coffee shop. Take a moment and notice how often men **leer** at women these days. What you witness there will likely confirm what you are reading here.

Zombies exhibit ravenous hunger. As zombies feed on human flesh (which is what porn does), internal fires rage and desire becomes ravenous. It's as if consuming creates the urge to consume more. Lastly, relationships are realigned. They become disrupted.

Where we once walked with and enjoyed others, we now feed on and destroy others. Over time, as zombies feed on the flesh of others, they cannibalize themselves and rot from the inside out.

Clearly the signs of the apocalypse are upon us!

Emphatically, porn is making zombies of us all!

Once desire is distorted and disrupted by pornography addiction, then disengagement and disembodiment become the normative, common experience.

Number 3: The End Game of Disengagement, Fostered by Porn, is Disembodiment!

The movie, *Warm Bodies*, vividly portrays porn's end game, which is disengagement and disembodiment. *Warm Bodies* follows the life of a young man who is almost fully dehumanized. In other words, he has succumbed to zombification (yes, that's a word). His name is **"R."** He narrates the movie.

In the opening scene, R makes an attempt to account for what led to the walking-dead world he now inhabits. He guesses it might have been chemical warfare, airborne virus, a radioactive outbreak, etc. He fails to understand the original cause. In this scene, R flashes back to the pre-zombie, human world. We hear him wistfully reflect,

"It must have been so much better before. People being able to connect, able to share their feelings and just enjoy each other's company."

Brilliantly, the movie depicts a scene where humans are doing the opposite of what R dreams they once did. Rather than connecting, they are disconnected and trapped within themselves. Rather than enjoying each other's company, they are fully disengaged.

In a brief moment of recollection we see a host of people in a crowded space similar to a mall. In this space, however, all are alone and none are connecting. Heads are down, shoulders are slumped, and thumbs are frantically gyrating over their smart phones. Humans are depicted as zombies - techno zombies, of sorts. This scene leads one to surmise that the warfare that caused the apocalypse was not chemical but technological.[x] Our addictions (in this case smartphones) foster disengagement and disengagement births disembodiment.

Our culture has a multitude of disengagement pathways from which to choose (iPod, iPads, smartphones, social-media apps, etc.). Data from a multitude of sources affirms that pornography continues to be the most dominant among them, utilizing technology as a gateway of sorts.[xi]

Before I continue, I invite you to pause and consider the following questions. They are designed to help assess one's degree of relational detachment:

1. Do you have trouble looking into the eyes of those you love?
2. Do your emotional triggers always fire?
3. Do you experience sudden outbursts of anger, inexplicable fear, or anxiety?
4. Do the night hours prove to be a restless experience?
5. Do you linger in-and-out of a state of shallow-sleep?
6. Do you often fight the urge to medicate, escape into your fantasy world?
7. Do you fear being exposed?

8. Do you wonder if you deleted that link or discarded that text?
9. Are you constantly "looking over your shoulder" to be sure you have covered your tracks?

An affirmative answer to two or more of these might signal a pattern of disengagement. This indicates you have ceased to function in the inherently human way of building upon and leaning into the relationships and moments of your life. As such, relationships and moments designed to solidify your place, purpose, and presence in this world are becoming nonexistent.

Indeed, disembodiment has begun.

Beyond these personal manifestations of disembodiment, we are noticing cultural (even global) dispositions likely fostered by addiction related to pornography.

For example, consider the following cultural and **global** realities:

1. **A Disposition to Violence and Conflict.**

From the playgrounds to the policy makers, conflict, power, control, bullying, manipulation, and smear are becoming normative ways of relating. Our boys are becoming more violent, and our daughters are disappearing daily. Indeed, we are all zombies now. We now have empirical evidence to support the connection between porn addiction and violence and rape.[xii]

2. **Relational and Familial Conflicts.**

I've experienced this in my personal life, and I have seen it dozens of time over the course of my ministry. Porn leads to conflict, insecurity, emotional bondage, self-absorption, disengagement, and an overall feeling of distrust. Such anecdotal evidence is now being supported by studies indicating that porn addiction has made marriage less desirable and secure and brought more harm, destruction, and conflict to marriage and other meaningful relationships.[xiii]

I have shared my story of struggling through porn addiction in a variety of settings. In every one of them I have never found anyone who *enjoys* being addicted to porn. I do find that men are reluctant to admit or confess their addiction, but once their eyes are opened, they all - to a person - want to be set free. Your marriage can be better and YOU can be the reason! Your relationships can improve and your engagement in them can provide the hope they need. You must first admit you have a problem and then reach out for help.

3. **Premature Ejaculation, Impotence, and an Inability to Control Sexual Urges (euphemistically known as "erectile dysfunction").**

Erectile Dysfunction, we are finding, is a painful and pervasive outcome of the porn industry's prolific reach. Ironically, the porn industry and they who support it have advanced the notion that porn can help your sexual experiences and actually make them more enjoyable. This is a flagrant falsehood which is now being exposed through scientific data and medical industry patterns.[xiv]

Here is the deal: if you struggle with impotence (let's just call it what it is) and you routinely watch or view porn, then the problem is not in your pants, it's in your head.

You are entertaining images that actually contribute to the loss of libido vitality. While you may need medicine, you most need intervention. You - we all - need help to stop. I promise you this: you cannot stop viewing porn on your own.

4. **The METEORIC Rise of Rape and Sexual Assault.**

When one of the most profitable industries on the planet generates its revenue via the objectification of persons (particularly women), the natural outcome will be things like rape, murder, and vicious crimes of hate. Often ignored by our pundits and cultural commentators is the growing unease of the generation coming behind us. It's as if they have clothed themselves in a hair-trigger culture screaming toward conflict. This hair-trigger culture is, in my opinion, the natural outcome of a people hooked on and consumed by pornography. The resulting dehumanization and distortion are evident to all who have eyes to see. The presence of this *hair-trigger, conflict-bound culture* is being reported on college campuses across this country.

Between the years of 2008 - 2012 college campuses reported a 49% increase in rape. One in four female undergrads reports being sexually abused and/or assaulted while incapacitated or held against their will. We can draw a direct line from porn addiction to rape, and it's simply appalling that so many of us remain in denial.[xv]

I have a daughter. I hope to, one day, have granddaughters. I have two sons. I hope to, one day, have grandsons. Statistics like these send a shiver down my spine. I am alarmed about the type of culture I am leaving behind and have decided to do all I can to bring this evil to light and contend with anyone who arrogantly - and in the most cavalier of ways - would attempt to tell me porn is not a global epidemic eating out the core of our soul. If you think this is bad, just wait until you read the next staggering by-product porn has given our world.

5. The Global Travesty of Sex Trafficking and the Modern Slave Trade.

The third largest criminal industry in the world is the buying and selling of humans. Porn does, we are finding, play a dishearteningly impressive role in the buying and selling of humans.[xvi]

It's a simple as this: With every click we claim another captive!

No society, in any land, can withstand the crushing weight of such human indignity and exploitation. We will collapse under the weight of this systemic and structural injustice if we don't take steps to alleviate this problem and provide a pathway to freedom for those forced into slave labor.

We can do better. We must do better. The end of sex trafficking begins with a commitment to end porn, period!

As you can see, when patterns of porn addiction are repeated in our homes, neighborhoods, cubicles, and classrooms, we foster a world of disengagement that leads to the experience of disembodiment. In other words, Porn addiction is the dehumanization of humanity. Porn is the end of the world! A world where the disengaged disembody.

I'm no scientist or sociologist, but even the most caved in and cloistered among us would confess that *cultural disembodiment* is now the rule rather than the exception!

Clearly the signs of the Zombie Apocalypse are upon us.

WE ARE ALL ZOMBIES NOW: A WAKE-UP CALL FOR THOSE WHO ARE NOT ADDICTED

I have attempted to use our infatuation with Zombies as a metaphor for dehumanization. We must come to terms with the reality that we are all, in some sense, porn addicts. *Even though you may not struggle with pornography consumption - as a person living in this culture, you, too, are consumed by it.* Porn consumption is not simply a problem for the addict. It is a problem for all of us who allow such disembodiment to exist and who pretend it causes no harm.

Noticeably, pornography has reshaped the life-giving rhythms of human sexuality into experiences of sexual *objectification, domination, subjugation, and inequality*. These realities are experienced at nearly every turn and evidenced in nearly every form of pornography consumed on a daily, moment-by-moment, basis.

For example, porn's **contribution** to society - with bravado and cavalier arrogance - is to offer women as subjects to the sexual desires of men. Ironically, such female subjugation has given rise to the dominatrix, or female who wields the power and control. The dominatrix is, however, a gimmick (and insulting) answer to the problem of female subjugation and dismemberment by the porn industry. *Indeed, female subjugation holds pride of place in the porn industry and will continue to constitute the warp and woof of its enterprise.*[xvii]

In such a world, the experience of sexual pleasure becomes one of conflict and competition, bondage and control. We are living out one of the greatest ironies of human history:

The irony of a world which is seeking equality - rightly so - all the while perpetuating the fundamental rhythms of inequality in the most meaning-shaping moments of our lives.

The phenomenon of *50 Shades of Grey* is perhaps the most explicit example of the acceptance of sexual subjugation within mainstream cultural forces.

As I reflect on my past of porn consumption/addiction, I confess I cannot recall one moment of mutual consent.

In fact, the experience is discordant on every level. All too often the act is cloaked in power, domination, and self-absorption. In short order, it's all about consumption.

The consumer both consumes and is consumed! Porn consumption ignites an insatiable urge to consume the flesh of another. Once we cooperate with this desire, we are sacrificed on the altar of power, control, and self-inflicted slavery. Seemingly, a common characteristic of *zombie experience* is the insatiable desire to consume another human being, becoming less human with each bite!

Alas, one's fantasy world of porn consumption/addiction precedes one's social and cultural detachment, pushing all toward dehumanization. Once dehumanized, human relationship and interaction is retooled.

Others become ends designed to fit the means of personally and culturally distorted desires.

LEERY-EYED LEECHES

One need only visit a Starbucks or a nearby cafe. In short order, you will find this to be true: We are now a culture of leery-eyed leeches. We (men particularly) possess others as we longingly, ravenously leer at body parts rather than being held captive by another's eyes.

Women sense when they are prey!

They hate us for it. Rightly so.

A Zombie desires flesh to satisfy a repulsive and compulsive hunger. In such a perpetual objectification of humanity, we view others as something slightly less than human, becoming something slightly more than animal.

Indeed, we are all zombies now.

There is a way to reverse the current trajectory and re-establish a baseline of hope, renewal, and restoration.

This is the trajectory I have traveled and am currently traveling. I'll now turn my focus toward this trajectory in the hopes of inspiring you to believe that a porn-free life is possible.

3 CHAPTER 3: POWER OF THE GOSPEL

THE POWER OF THE GOSPEL AND THE JOY OF LIVING A PORN-FREE LIFE.

In I Peter 1:3 – 9 we read,

> *"May the God and Father of our Lord Jesus Christ be blessed! On account of his vast mercy, he has given us new birth. You have been born anew into a living hope through the resurrection of Jesus Christ from the dead. 4 You have a pure and enduring inheritance that cannot perish—an inheritance that is presently kept safe in heaven for you. 5 Through his faithfulness, you are guarded by God's power so that you can receive the salvation he is ready to reveal in the last time. 6 You now rejoice in this hope, even if it's necessary for you to be distressed for a short time by various trials. 7 This is necessary so that your faith may be found genuine. (Your faith is more valuable than gold, which will be destroyed even though it is itself tested by fire.) Your genuine faith will result in praise, glory, and honor for you when Jesus Christ is revealed. 8 Although you've never seen him, you love him. Even though you don't see him now, you trust him and so rejoice with a glorious joy that is too much for words. 9 You are receiving the goal of your faith: your salvation."*

This text paints a beautiful picture and casts a potent vision of the unending hope we have in the Gospel of God through Jesus Christ. Indeed, you and I have been born into a living hope. This rebirth gives us reason to celebrate, regardless of the momentary trial and/or temptation.

Anyone who has ever attempted to beat any addiction, particularly porn addiction, needs to hear and receive these life-giving words!

In order to begin our journey into freedom we must begin to live as the freedmen (people) we already are because of the resurrection of Christ our Lord.

Psalm 34:8 encourages us to *"taste and see that the Lord is good."* Another word for taste might be **meditate**, which means to chew over and over and over again.

Peter Leithhart, writing for the magazine, First Things, offers us a compelling explanation meditation:

"The word 'meditate' refers to a sound, the sound of muttering to oneself, the sound of whispered self-conversation. Or, the sound of a lion with its prey (Isaiah 31:4), the sound of thunder (Job 37:2), the sound of a harp (Psalm 9:16; 92:3) or of doves (Isaiah 38:14). Yahweh tells Joshua to growl over the word, protective as a lion; to rumble like a small thundercloud with the word in his mouth; to fill his mouth with the word so that he will become a musical instrument; to eat the book so that he coos like the dove of the Spirit."[xviii]

I'd encourage you to take heart in and meditate on Peter's encouraging verse.

Consider the following promises and affirmations in this powerful portion of Scripture found in I Peter 1:

God's mercy provides new birth, v.3.

Porn addiction brings death, or at least the experience of death and decay. The Gospel offers new birth. Remember, the birthing process is as grueling as it is beautiful!

Yet, there is always hope as the grace of the Gospel literally pushes us through the birthing canal into the fresh air of new-life and the hope that we can breathe-free once again!

Breathe air that's porn-free and full of freedom!

This new birth provides living hope, v.3.

As long as we have life, we have hope. We not only have life everlasting (tomorrow). The Gospel promises us life *today*. When Jesus showed up on the scene, he offered His new converts nothing less than hope!

When he says things like, "repent, the kingdom of heaven is at hand," it's as if He is saying, "*You're going the wrong way, doing the wrong thing. God is doing a new thing! Give up this path you are on. Get out of this rut you are in and follow me! I've got a path, I'm on a path, I AM the path that you're going to want to follow.*"

This is both the ground and goal of our hope! Notice also that this is a living hope. The form of the word implies on-going action and opportunity. The hope the Gospel brings simply cannot be imprisoned! It's always fresh. It's always new. It's always enough!

This living hope is achieved through the finished work of Christ, v. 4.

He has defeated death (and all its cousins like porn addiction) through the resurrection. The big-lie of porn is that it has convinced you that its power is greater than the power of Christ in and an among us. The Gospel, however, ensures us that there is no greater power in existence today. Certainly evil holds a degree of sway but it's on life-support. Jesus drained ever last ounce of energy out of the evil when He defeated it on the cross.

We might say that Jesus actually beat the death out of death.

This work is irreversible and as secure today as it was when it was first accomplished. Peter goes on to say that we **now** have an imperishable inheritance kept under safeguard in Heaven.

Trials test and prove our faith and give us cause to rejoice, v. 5 – 7.

Present struggles prove our faith genuine and provide a context in which our trust in Christ is strengthened. As our faith grows so grows our trust. Trust, in other words, is not contingent upon what we "see" but on whom we rely.

Such knowledge is invaluable. We often wonder, 'why, O Lord, do I still struggle so?" Reflections of this nature aren't grounded in the Gospel as much as they are in our own ingratitude. Peter reminds us that our struggle provides an opportunity for us to prove God's power again and again.

One of the most aggravating and profoundly imbecilic things I hear when I work with people (especially Christians) battling porn is the idea that you have to be perfect in order to be free. That's just a big-ole-pile-a pooh!

We must come to rest in the knowledge that we can be free and still fight! In fact, that's the entire testimony of Scripture! We have the power of Christ in and among us so that His power might live and breathe through us! We have his power in us so that He might achieve victory for us. Yes, you will likely struggle for the rest of your life, to one degree or another. It doesn't however mean that you're not free. It just means that you're honest!

It is this hope – the hope the Gospel, and the Gospel alone, affords – that I'll now turn my attention to. I will do so by presenting my portions of personal journey out of addiction and into a porn-free life. My journey is one of many ups and downs and a multitude of fits and starts. I've discovered that the will to change is not enough, and the power to change is not in me. Rather – meaningful, lasting, and transformative – change occurs as I trust in a Good and Beautiful God and practice rhythms and disciplines that enable me to abide in Him and remain connected to the life-giving power of His presence!

I've learned to draw from the power of The Gospel of God in Christ and power narratives and spiritual practices that continue to help me break free from porn and nurture a flourishing life that will blossom into full bloom!

As I said earlier, over time and through a set of repeated practices and habits, I began scrubbing the false narratives out of my life with true, or power, narratives.

Two power narratives (to rely on James Bryan Smith's terms) I have relied upon over the years are:

POWER NARRATIVE 1: I AM – IN CHRIST – ALWAYS ENOUGH.

The Apostle Paul prays this reminder over us in Ephesians 1 when he says,

"I pray that the eyes of your heart may be enlightened in order that you may know the hope to which he has called you, the riches of his glorious inheritance in his holy people, and his incomparably great power for us who believe. That power is the same as the mighty strength he exerted when he raised Christ from the dead and seated him at his right hand in the heavenly realms, far above all rule and authority, power and dominion, and every name that is invoked, not only in the present age but in the age to come."

POWER NARRATIVE 2: I CAN TRUST GOD: HE IS GOOD.

Psalm 27 reinforces this truth, "Teach me how to live, O Lord. Lead me along the right path. I am confident *I will see (or taste) the Lord's goodness while I am here in the land of the living*. Wait patiently for the Lord. Be brave and courageous. Yes, wait patiently for the Lord."

Power narratives contain inherent cleansing strength. They serve as strong correctives to the false narratives that porn exploits and perpetuates. Though I have only stumbled into Smith's writings in the last three years, I realize that the reason I have – and am – experiencing freedom from porn's grip is that *my focus of attention shifted from my sin and shame to the beauty of God*

AND the delight He takes when he looks at me! In other words, I began – long ago – to feed the power narratives of God's great love for me and starve the false narratives of porn's lusty allure over me. I continue to spend time meditating on them, praying over them, and believing in the truth they contain!

REFLECT, RESOLVE, RESTORE

Before we move on, I'd like to invite you to take a few moments and consider the narratives that guide your life. Are they narratives of life-giving freedom (power narratives) that have been formed and shaped by the Gospel of God in Christ?

Or are they narratives of life-stealing entrapment (false narratives) that have been formed and shaped by the painful and distorted rhythms of an unloved, unwanted life?

Once you identify a few, share them with a trusted friend and begin the process of walking with someone toward the freedom and restoration which is yours to enjoy!

If you are trapped in the pain of porn's pulsating grip, please hear me: There is hope. You do not have to stay trapped. My journey will not be yours, but it may provide some checkpoints by which you can measure where you are and where you are heading.

These days, after long stints of travel or hectic seasons of life and ministry where Melissa and I find ourselves separated from mutual embrace, I find that I long to return to her embrace rather than run toward porn's pull. I return to her – again and again – as a man who is free from the grip of a once-painful and all-consuming problem.

Why?

Because - over time and through intention - I began to see myself as God sees me and focused on His truth and the person I am in Him. I am free from porn's powerful grip. I have been for many years now. I am, of course, still tempted. But its power over me has diminished. That I can make such a claim is a testimony to the power of the Gospel of God in Christ and the wonder and joy found in the warm embrace of His love.

I am not sure where you are on your journey out of porn. Perhaps you are captured, perhaps you are complacent. If either one is true you are, as am I, less complete. There is more yet to come, and it will require help.

There continue to be – to this very day – forces at work inside of me that I don't fully understand. I find that, when those forces fire, I revert to practicing the rhythms of dysfunction rather than freedom. In those moments, I **run** back to the basics – basics of individual and corporate spirituality that we will turn our attention to now. I like the guy I become when I return to the basics. He's free and, as it turns out, others like him, too.

4 RECOGNIZING AND RESPONDING TO YOUR UNIQUE TRAPS AND TRIGGERS

LEARNING HOW TO AVOID TEASING SENSATION, TEMPTING SITUATION, AND THE TRAP-DAY

I struggled with porn addiction for years before I realized that certain moments, thoughts, people, or places were triggers that ignited my desire and drove my decision-making process. I *know them now*, and I have to be ready for them.

A couple of trigger and traps are:

1. Seasons of life that are particularly demanding and/or taxing.
2. Transitions in life such as a new place of work or a new move.
3. Moments or days after I have expended a large amount of emotional energy on a task or project.

Any of the moments described above are potential triggers and traps that can trick me into believing porn is a necessary escape.

I am not sure what your triggers and traps are, but I know you have them. So, I am going present four areas of potential triggers and traps in the hope that reading them will awaken you to and keep you aware of your own.

In my own journey, awareness of these triggers and traps has provided firm footing on which to stand and has enabled me to live a robust and wonderfully healthy post-porn addiction life!

Triggers and Traps

1. **The Trying Season.** The American Psychological Association reports that nearly 70% of us believe stress has an impact on our physical well-being.[xix] I wonder if we realize the

impact of stress on our mental and emotional health? While stress is the norm for many, highly stressful seasons of life are the experience of every one of us.

Consider two dominant areas of life experience:

1. **Relational.** This is life with friends or family, pending life stage and development.

2. **Work/Education.** This is the area of life that likely occupies most of your time. For those in a career, it means a job. For those who are students it means school work, life and all the activities that come with being a student in your typical academic setting.

In both areas, ***relationships and work***, formation and deformation are happening all the time. For example: when you work hard and receive a promotion or pay raise, you experience formation. Your energies are rewarded and recognized by your colleagues, which gives you a sense of pride and accomplishment.

The experience of pride and accomplishment help form our sense of ***personhood, plac'dness, and purpose*** in our world. In moments like these, ones of value, esteem and recognition, something sacred is at work. It's as if places in us – often places we aren't even aware exist – are being shaped and formed.

In such moments, we experience joy and fulfillment. While this is a beautiful moment that brings hope, it is also accompanied by subtle but certain stressors.

Intuitively, we begin to entertain thoughts like these:

Wow, what is this going to do for my career in the long run?

More success, more money, more stuff, more hours at work?

What's my spouse going to think about this?

Does this mean I have to put in that pool he has been

nagging me to put in these past two years?

How will this impact my relationship with my colleagues?

Yes. Even in moments of joy and celebration, stress begins to build. Most of the stress is, of course, self-inflicted, but that's not the point. The point is that stress begins to build during moments we would not expect it to build. If we don't awaken to this reality, it will grow over time and become the dominate narrative from which we live.

Soon, we are in the midst of a **Trying Season** and we aren't quite sure how we even got there.

As stress builds anxiety increases.

As anxiety increases, frustration takes hold.

As frustration takes hold, conflict – both internal and external – grows.

As conflict grows, stress becomes the norm.

When stress becomes the norm, we sense a growing need to escape reality and relieve all the tension. The Trying Season then falls prey to porn's opportunistic pull and we act out.

We click that web page that offers total satisfaction with very little investment.

We hunt, really scour, the World Wide Web. Hoping to find that caring companion who will, for just a small amount of our hard-earned money, ease away the pain, if only for a while.

We stroll into that massage parlor that everyone knows offers more than back rubs and seek to receive a solace our stressed out lives fail to provide.

You get the picture.

Porn's power is weaponized in the midst of Trying Seasons and stressful realities.

For any who have struggled with porn, we know that such behavior actually leads us to shame and guilt, only adding to the stress we were trying to relieve. In the space of such self-created tension, we begin to lash out at those we love and they who love us.

First we lash out ourselves, then take it out on our spouse, then we randomly and carelessly yell and scream at the kids.

Finally, we retreat into an isolated island of Self-loath and despair, wondering if we will ever be free. Hoping, really, that we would one day be able to at least put up a fight.

Indeed, if we are not careful the Trying Season will lead to moments of self-induced, relationship-crushing pain.

Take hope.

This need not be the case.

There are health-creating steps we can take before running to porn and compounding our stress:

1. **Awaken to and become aware of internal stressors.** The way I do this is by pausing a few times a day and then at least once or twice a week and reflecting on how I feel. It's helpful for me to identify the emotions stirring within my soul. Am I angry? Am I sad? Am I nervous? Am I concerned, etc.?

2. **Accept responsibility for my emotions.** It's easy for me to blame others for my feelings. This rarely helps. If I can accept responsibility for my emotions, then I can take positive steps to empower myself and direct my emotions back toward health.

3. **Ask a friend for help and/or counsel.** The journey out of addiction is not a journey you can take alone. Reach out to a trusted

friend, spouse, brother, sister, counselor, pastor, mentor, coach.

4. **Alter the trajectory of your thought life.** This is crucial. You simply have to 'get out of your head.' That ongoing conversation of how everyone is against you is as unhelpful as it is untrue. Once you nurture and cultivate a toxic thought-life, you are setting yourself up for addictive behavior. Begin to speak truth and spend time with those who will speak truth to and with you!

We experience life-giving and life-taking moments throughout all of our lives. That's why being aware of and awake to the trying and stressful seasons is critical if you are going to break free from porn's pull.

If you are a porn addict or significantly struggle to stay away from porn's pull, then this season is one of which you need to be aware.

The steps I have offered may or may not work for you. In fact, you may have some of your own. If so, please let us know what they are so we can provide them for others who are on this journey as well.

I will now reflect on three other realities porn seeks to exploit and ways I have learned to live porn-free in their midst. They are:

1. The Teasing Sensation.
2. The Tempting Situations.
3. The Trap Day.

The Teasing Sensation

Life is full of teasers.

A teaser is, according to Merriam-Webster, "something that is done, offered, or shown to *make people want something* or want to see something that will be offered or shown at a later time."

Teasers, or teasing sensations, pose significant challenges for at least two reasons:

- **We don't expect them.** They can show up out of nowhere and grab a hold of the addict's heart with ferocious power.
- **We cannot control or anticipate our initial response to them.** Usually, the response if full of energy and excitement that seems almost uncontrollable. Fortunately, it's not uncontrollable!

Yes, teasers present a host of problems. Teasers, or teasing sensations, are often leveraged by the Trying Season, Tempting Situations and The Trap Day – all triggers and traps this series is designed to help us fight!!

Invariably, they become the fertile soil in which porn addiction and consumption seek to take root and grow!

Consider the following teasers you and I might encounter during an average day:

1. A 'pop up' add on your computer.
2. A commercial during your favorite program.
3. A movie trailer at the local theater.
4. A flirty glance or accidental – but charged - touch from a colleague.
5. A magazine cover at the ten-item aisle in your local grocery store.
6. A girl at your local gym.

You get the point. From Starbucks to the grocery store, teasers, or the teasing sensation, occur randomly and unexpectedly and we can NEVER control our initial emotional response.

Let me free you from that trap. You know the trap that takes your initial excitement or rush of energy and makes you feel like dirt? Men and women are creatures of desire. We – all of us – want. We want deeply so. If *longing and desire* were not central to what it means to be human, then teasers would gain no ground!

So, if you see someone dressed in a way that stimulates you, or if you are caught off guard by an advertisement that excites you, relax -

that's okay – *don't let your initial reaction lead you to a place of destruction and pain.*

It's just a reaction, a reflex. Do you remember when your doctor used to whack your knee with a rubber hammer? Try as you might, as a kid, you couldn't stop your knee from responding. Our emotions work in similar ways. They respond to stimulus and stimulating moments.

The enemy of our soul and society seeks to distort godly desire and tease us into a tempting situation. The forces that rule the porn empire know that once one *is teased into a tempting situation*, it becomes all too easy to click that website and feed the addiction!

The question is, for those of us who want to be porn-free,

"What actions or steps can we take AFTER that initial reflex and response?"

"What can we do to ensure that the emotional response doesn't digress into a normative way of life and living?"

Here are a few suggestions from my life. I share them not in triumph, but from tragedy. These ideas were birthed in the midst of despair and pain. They are, however, tried and true ways I become aware of and awake to the realities of living in a world bent on Trying, Teasing, and Tempting.

Preparing For and Responding to the Teasing Sensation

1. **Anticipate teasing sensations and situations and make a plan for how you will respond in that moment.** I simply sat down one day and wrote out all the possible times the teasing sensation might occur. After jotting down eight to ten of them, I developed some ways I would respond in those moments. I sought to develop life-giving, hope-birthing rhythms of response

rather than shame-filled, guilt-ridden mechanisms of despair.

2. **Share the moments with a loved one or accountability partner.** Share them quickly. I find that verbally expressed the sensation reduces its power and pull in my mind and heart. Speaking it to another person proves to be wonderfully healing!

3. **Get out of the situation and away from the sensation!** Getting away from the teasing sensation may mean avoiding my computer, leaving the coffee shop, closing or 'bouncing' my eyes, etc. If I remain in the moment and entertain the sensation, I give it the power to move me toward temptation.

4. **Negative reinforcement can bring me back to reality.** During my initial season or stages of recovery, these moments posed powerful and anxiety producing situations. I found it helpful to wrap a rubber band around my left hand. When such moment occurred, I would snap the band, producing an immediate and equal negative response to the sensation. I would then think of my wife and the joy I have in her, which reinforced a positive affirmation of my identity and sense of personhood.

The Tempting Situation

As I write this portion on preparing for and resisting **The Tempting Situation**, I am sitting in a Starbucks drinking my customary Grande Bold Coffee, black.

Here is what I can tell you based on this *one morning* in Starbucks: For those of us who are trying to live a porn-free life, or who are trying to maintain a porn-free life, temptations abound, and they are everywhere.

We will, at some point, be tempted or face a **Tempting Situation**, in which our desires to click on a porn link or website will be tugged and cajoled – many times more than once a day.

Often, more than once an hour.

Yes. If you've battled the soul-wrenching beast of porn addiction, you know exactly what I'm talking about!

Facing temptations, or the **Tempting Situation**, is a reality with which we must all come to grips.

The irony of writing this - about resisting the **Tempting Situation** - in a Starbucks, is that I am going to suggest we consider a picture from an ancient writer, Homer, to help us prepare for and resist temptation. The work to which I am referring is found in Books 12 – 14 of his Epic, The Odyssey.

Tempting Situations and the Long Journey Home

By way of summation, Odysseus and his crew are on their voyage home, after the Trojan Wars. During this lengthy journey home, he and his shipmates sail past the Isle of Sirens (thus the irony, as Starbucks' logo is based on a Siren), where the famed daughters of the gods await, singing their silky songs of seduction.

The Sirens' objective is to tempt the crew to take a detour and investigate the beautiful shores of the island they inhabit. The Sirens make promises they cannot – and have no intention to – fulfill. They promise Odysseus and his crew passion, pleasure, and gratification, knowing they will deliver distortion, destruction, and, ultimately, death.

The crew, in other words, faces a **Tempting Situation** that's filled with power and persuasion but will end in distortion and destruction. The Isle of Sirens' power is found only in its persuasion, not in its intention or ability to deliver what's promised.

Consider this gripping stanza and the stark reality of how the sultry sounds of the Sirens would lead to death and death alone:

> *Their song is death, and makes destruction please.*
> *Unblest the man, whom music wins to stay*
> *Nigh the cursed shore and listen to the lay.*
> *No more that wretch shall view the joys of life*

His blooming offspring, or his beauteous wife![xx]

The line that grabs my heart, "*No more that wretch shall view the joys of life*," describes how terribly wrecked life becomes when one gives in to the **Tempting Situation**. I have been there on more than one occasion. You know, that place where we experience the wretchedness of giving into porn's sultry song.

In all likelihood, you've been there as well. Indeed, to give in to the **Tempting Situation** the Isle of Sirens poses, is to give the temptation power over our life. It's a power that leaves us awash on a shore of guilt and shame.

When we give in to temptation, we experience detachment and disengagement from those people who love is the most and in those places where our life finds the most meaning!! No more do we enjoy the wonders of life found in our spouse, children, extended community, and vocation.

The porn industry has taken a page or two from Greek mythology, offering the hope of satisfaction while delivering the reality of suffocation.

The sights and sounds of the Tempting Situation are often enticing. Of course, if they weren't enticing, there would be no need to prepare or resist. So, how do we prepare for and resist the many **Tempting Situations** that we face on a daily basis?

After all, Sirens abound in today's porn-saturated world.

Consider the following ways I battle the ongoing reality of temptation in today's *Isle-of-Sirens society*:

A Few Ways to Prepare for and Resist the Tempting Situation

1. Be Prepared!

Accept the reality that the **Tempting Situation** is going to present itself. I don't care how many days, weeks, months, or years you've been porn-free, you will still be tempted. There is nothing wrong with being tempted; it's how you respond in the **Tempting Situation** that determines the immediate outcomes. It's important that you develop a list of **Triggers and Traps** that are specific to you and your own struggle.

2. Be Intentionally Preventative!

Take preventative steps so that you can resist when you face the **Tempting Situation**! Odysseus and his crew prepared for the **Tempting Situation** the Isle would present by taking steps – ahead of time - to resist the tempting Island. The crew plugged their ears and covered their eyes. Odysseus himself was tied to the mast to prevent him from giving in to the sultry sounds of the Sirens' tempting song.

3. Build a Team!

Find a community of people whom you can trust and upon whom you can rely when the **Tempting Situation** occurs. Porn's **Tempting Situations** exploit isolation and fatigue. Ongoing participation in and with a community of others who struggle in this way will play a crucial role in your ability to resist when the Sirens sound their song!!

4. Behold True Beauty.

While this is last on the list, it's the most important. A vision of beauty around the joy of being home is life-giving and provides power when faced with the Tempting Situation. In other words, our desire to be with the ones we love and those who love us – fully engaged – is the place where our resistance begins!

The only way I've been able to resist the tempting trinkets of porn's lust-filled, soul-sapping world, is by beholding the true and life-giving beauty already present in my life! Odysseus holds fast because he has a vision of being at home. He has beheld the beauty of his loving wife and longs to be captivated by the beauty he beholds.

The **Tempting Situation** presented by porn, conversely, pounds the love out of us and strips us of the beauty we desperately long to behold!

Odysseus was compelled to 'stay the course' because his true love – his beauty beheld - *awaited* his return.

As I sip my last sip of morning joe, I do so from a cup that reminds me there are Sirens all around and, as such, I must be prepared and ready to resist the **Tempting Situation**. I am also encouraged by the reality that the Siren song, though a reality in our world, loses its power of persuasion as I lean into and live out the suggestions above!

What has become a reality for me is also possible for you!

Be encouraged. Reflect on and implement just one step above and try to take it one moment at a time!

The Trap-Day

I know the term **Trap-Day** is an unfamiliar one. It is, in fact, not one I have heard of anywhere else. That's because it's one that is birthed from my personal journey out of porn addiction and into a porn-free life. In my experience the **Trap-Day** is *a day of ongoing struggle with porn's pull. It's a day when one is particularly susceptible to porn and its destructive power of persuasion.*

The **Trap-Day** is as unexpected as it is unavoidable.

The **Trap-Day** is debilitating because it is durative.

While the term may be new to you, the experience I am describing is likely all too familiar. It's the experience of being stuck in your addiction and – seemingly – unable to break free. You can break free, though. Before I discuss how it's possible to live porn – free in the troughs of the **Trap-Day**, I am going to identify a couple of

Trap-Day characteristics. Identifying some characteristics may help you recognize, prepare for, and resist this day in your life.

Characteristics of the Trap-Day

1. **A Day of Adrenaline Depletion/Depression.** The trap day typically appears immediately following a day in which one has expended a vast amount of emotional, mental, physical and spiritual energy. In other words, the **Trap-Day** assails when one is worn-out and too weak to put up a strong resistance.

Because of my personal weekly rhythms, the **Trap-Day** always falls on a Monday. It can, however, occur at any time and always shows up when I am deeply drained and in need of rest!

The **Trap-Day** for you may not be weekly. Paying attention to your daily and weekly schedule will help you begin to recognize the **Trap-Day** and prepare for ways to endure it.

2. **A Day that Seizes Relapse or Accentuates Failure.** The **Trap-Day** is a master at making one feel like a failure. It's a day in which the memory of the prolific nature of a past with porn and the pain it causes is all too real.

The **Trap-Day** may exploit the ways in which triggers have, recently, been entertained, rather than resisted. I have found that, in the midst of the **Trap-Day**, old memories – many years old – grab a hold of my heart and mind in a painful way. Of course, it's all a lie. But, in the moment, when enduring is difficult, it seems true and serves as a reminder of how difficult this journey is.

Even though porn addiction is no longer true of me, the power of memory combined with the moment of weakness is difficult – but not impossible – to fight against!

Though the **Trap-Day** cannot be avoided, it can be endured. It can also become a day in which one can experience great victory and freedom. The key to victory over the **Trap-Day** is found in whom or what we *behold*, rather than how we hope to behave.

I call this key the **Practice or Rhythm of Beholding True Beauty**!

To behold is to *"reflect upon, look upon, gaze upon or consider often and regularly."*

In my journey out of porn and into a porn-free life, the true beauty I choose to behold – on a regular and consistent basis, shapes the inner realities of my heart. These inner, or core, realities, shape me in such a way that – in moments of undeniable weakness and unavoidable temptation – I am able to stand strong and live from this place of beauty.

Beholding True Beauty

As I practice the rhythm of **Beholding True Beauty**, I find that true beauty beholds me. In other words, beauty – true beauty – is life giving. Life-giving is the antithesis of what porn offers. Porn is the distortion of beauty.

Reflect on the following options for a **True Beauty to Behold**:

Behold the beauty of God.

Psalm 27:4 – 5 is one of my favorite passages of Scripture in this regard. The Psalmist exclaims,

*"One thing I ask from the Lord, this only do I seek: that I may dwell in the house of the Lord all the days of my life, to gaze on the beauty of the **Lord** and to seek him in his temple. 5 For in the day of trouble he will keep me safe in his dwelling; he will hide me in the shelter of his sacred tent and set me high upon a rock."*

Later in the Psalm we read, *"I remain confident of this: I will gaze on the goodness of the Lord in the land of the living."* This wonderful phrase is one that I memorize and hide in my heart so that its hope will hold me in the midst of the **Trap-Day** which is sure to come!

Behold the beauty of your spouse.

I have found that the **Trap-Day** tries to trick me into believe that I am not loved and/or cared for in the ways that I find meaningful and life-giving. If I buy this line, then the offering is a quick trip to porn and a speedy descent to destruction. I have learned to think and speak truth about my spouse and reflect on the moments when I have sensed her love.

I find that the more I behold the beauty of my spouse the less I give in to the power of porn's pull. Even better, the less I give in to the power of porn's pull, the more I am able to behold the beauty of my spouse. This rhythm leads to a literal *flywheel of freedom*.

Behold the beauty of your children.

I became serious about trying to deal with my porn addiction after the birth of our first son. Yes, I had attempted to shake it before his birth, but the reality that I would pass this sin onto him was weighty. Beholding the beauty of my children has always held me fast in the midst of the **Trap-Day**!

Behold the beauty of community and creation.

One of my favorite themes in The Odyssey (see above) theme of brothers who fight wars – of all kinds - together. Enduring the **Trap-Day** requires dependence on and commitment to a larger community of trusted friends who will speak truth into your life in a moment's notice.

The evil one, whom I believe is the father of porn, will twist you like a pretzel if he catches you alone and lonely! Don't give him the opportunity. Find – at the very least – one or two people who will walk with you and be there for you in your day of need!

I live close to a coast line so the Atlantic Ocean is within ten minutes of my home. If, during the rigors of the **Trap-Day**, I get out and experience the majesty of God's good creation, I find that the pressures of temptation decrease and the joy of freedom becomes attainable.

Behold the beauty of you!

This is as difficult as it is important. When self-doubt creeps into my mind and heart, insecurity begins to take root in my soul. As soon as insecurity takes root, porn's pull becomes nearly impossible to resist. I, therefore, have learned to practice the rhythm of being thankful to God for the innate gifts, desires and experience He has given me. This is closely related to, yet distinct from, beholding the beauty of vocation.

One of my favorite Bible verses to chew is found in Psalm 139:13 – 14, where the Psalmist proclaims,

> "You made all the delicate, inner parts of my body and knit me together in my mother's womb. ***Thank you for making me so wonderfully complex! Your workmanship is marvelous—how well I know it.***"

What a great reminder to me – especially when in enduring the **Trap-Day** – of the worth and value I hold in the eyes of our creator!

5 DEVELOPING FAMILY PROTOCOLS AND PREVENTION

PROTECTING YOUR CHILDREN FROM PORN

"How can I prevent my children from seeing porn?"

The above question is one I often hear. It's on the heart of every well-meaning and concerned parent these days. My answer to them is this: "You can't prevent your children from seeing porn. Eventually, they will see it."

I follow that up by encouraging them that there are ways to prepare their children for this eventuality and preparing them in their desire to **push back against porn** when it encroaches!!

Simple And Effective Ways Parents, Families, and Individuals Can Push Back Against Porn

Understand that *Porn is targeting our children.* This is crucial. Most parents don't realize how aggressive the porn industry is and how invasive it has become. The tactics and strategies the industry uses to suck pre-teens in are as pervasive as they are effective.

Well over two-thirds of a child's initial exposure to porn is unsolicited and unwelcomed.[xxi]

Preempt Porn's Perversion with Positive, encouraging, and life-giving parenting. Spend time with your children – both formally and informally – discussing the realities of porn in our world. Let them know that if, and when, they look at porn, that it is okay for them to tell you. In fact, they should know – without a doubt – that you want them to tell you!

After the initial thrill that porn provides begins to wane, fear and shame quickly settle in. Fear and shame are the soil in which isolation and silence are birthed. A child who stays choked by the roots of this silence and shame will – undoubtedly – run to porn again. This return to porn begins the slow but steady descent into addiction. Be preemptive!

Model Sexual Integrity. There is an old axiom that drips with truth: *More is caught than taught.* In the area of sexual wholeness this is certainly true. If you're married, then love your spouse above all other loves. Cherish your spouse and be sure your children know that.

Porn is fake love, and when you place it next to genuine marital love, it will always crumble. If you're single, then practice the type of sexual integrity you hope your children would model. I find that many men continue to secretly struggle with porn. If this is the case, then admit it. You don't have to tell your child, but you do need to share your addiction with a trusted friend and – sooner than later – your spouse.

Develop an *On-Going* Action Plan. Make some decisions regarding technology and how and when it will be used in your home. If your son or daughter has a smart phone, then you will need to establish a baseline of acceptable behavior that will protect them from the industry's reach.

Some things you might consider:
- Using a filter on all devices.[xxii]
- Check ALL history daily. When history is deleted, there will need to be consequences.
- No screens behind closed doors. For example, no

televisions, smart phones, tablets, or computers, etc. should be allowed behind closed doors such as bathrooms and bedrooms.

These are just a few suggestions that we've used in our home. You will need to establish some ground rules that work well within the preexisting flow of your family. No ground rules, however, is sure to lead to porn consumption, if not all-out addiction. Smart phones are pocket-sized perversion centers, and the porn industry both knows and exploits this reality thousands of times a minute. Silence and a failure to develop a technology-use plan is akin to aiding and abetting the porn industry

Don't be Afraid to Reach Out For Help

When I began my journey out of porn there were precious few resources. These days help can be found in nearly every community.

I hope for, pray for, and work toward the day in which our children do not have to grow up with the reality of pornography. This, however, is not that day. Until that day arrives, I will do all I can to help prevent porn's spread and prepare on others how to face it!

My wife and I - having three teenagers in our home - are raising children who are fully absorbed into the first technology-drenched generation. As such, we've learned a few things – often through failure – that might help those of you who are walking in – or are about to walk in – our shoes.

So, from the heart of one parent to another – if you are interested in PARENTING AGAINST PORN and guarding your child's heart, then take a minute and consider the following FIVE QUICK TIPS.

1. Wait as long as you can before giving your child a 'smart phone.'

Placing a smartphone in the hands of pre-teens and young teens is akin to breathing a virus over them and telling them not to inhale.

We're All Zombies Now

Ridiculous. We failed on this point. We've paid the price. I know the surrounding culture suggests every child needs a phone by the age of 8. That's just false. Resist this, as long as you can.

I'd suggest engaging your child in a meaningful conversation and then finding resources to aid you and your child as you prepare for the day when you do allow that first smartphone.

Wondering if I'm right? Think of it this way: would you take your child to a strip club and expose them to the environment therein? Or, would you sit down and watch an X-rated movie with them? Probably not. Smartphones are pocket sized peep shows that open your child to a world of relentless distraction, dehumanizing distortion, and ultimately, soul-sapping destruction.

2. No screens behind closed doors, ever.

This is a must. My wife and I, again, have learned the hard way. When you try to implement this one, you are likely to hear a barrage of the following arguments (there must be a web page where they come up with this stuff):

    a. But I need it for my homework.
    b. I'm just listening to music.
    c. Yeah, but it's my alarm clock.
    d. No other parent makes their kids do this.
    e. What about your phone, dad?

And the hits just keep on coming!

For every excuse, there's any easy and healthy alternative. Parents simply need resolve to see this one through. As one who has 'been there and done that,' and has failed as often as I've succeeded, I can tell you that this is a moment-by-moment, day-by-day, night-by-night reality.

Wondering why your teenage son spends inordinate amounts of time using the bathroom? *Come on, dad and mom.* Engage with me on this one. Keep the phones in common areas. Remember, this is not about parental authority as much as it is protecting our most valuable treasures – a child's heart!

3. Casual Check – ins Can Lead to Meaningful, Life-Shaping Moments.

This realization has changed the entire tenor of our home. If children - especially in their preteen and teen years - are approached only when we are concerned about something, they begin to develop patterns of defense and preservation for those moments.

My wife and I learned to seize the causal moments life often provides, but parents rarely see. Moments when the kids are engaged in something they like to do. Whether it is basketball or guitar, tossing a baseball or swimming in the pool, we've learned to take advantage of our time: doing some *causal check-ins* with our kids.

Now, as they are all teenagers, we both try to take our kids out to dinner once every couple of months, with no agenda. We just want to be with them.

Moments like this dig deep wells of trust that will provide refreshing waters of hope when your children experience troubles and trials that are sure to come their way!

4. Establish a System of Family-Wide Parameter and Permissions.

Every parameter we put on our kids are parameters we're willing to share as adults. We do this because our participation with them conveys the depth of our love for them and concern for their flourishing.

For example, if I enact a regulation for my child's good (look both ways before crossing the road), then the same regulation, should theoretically, be for my good as well.

Of course, there are exclusions to this, but even those are decided as a family.

5. Teach this: Sex is a Good, Glorious and God-given Gift.

Porn is not – and NEVER can be – sex. It's a distortion of sex and, as such, leads to disfigurement in life. I believe that porn capitalizes on our reluctance to teach the goodness and glory of sex.

We are wired for Eros. We are, fundamentally, erotic beings. In other words, we are wired to love and be loved. Eros is a beautiful biblical term. Within its beautiful boundaries, the sexual experience is one that brings delight and restores design.

Outside of its beautiful boundaries, the sexual experience (or quasi-sexual experience proffered by porn) brings distortion and ends in despair.

Early on, in our children's life, we emphasized the reality that sex is a gift from God to be shared in a meaningful and life-long covenant relationship. We have further taught them that the naked body is beautiful and, as such, it's a natural attraction.

However, porn asks us to view the naked bodies of those who aren't in a covenant relationship with us, and those who are being objectified (turned into tools to be used to fill someone's distorted desires) and dehumanized.

There is no battle more important than the fight to protect our child's heart and to guard them against the onslaught of a porn-saturated culture.

> *A recent study conducted by the NSPCC ChildLine found that a tenth of 12 to 13-year-olds fear they may be addicted to pornography. That's right, a whopping 10% of kids who just started 7th grade are saying they are already watching porn to the point where they are concerned and don't feel like they can stop. Why is this happening, and why at such an early age? It's all about accessibility and desensitization.*[xxiii]

Children, it seems, are finding, absorbing and becoming addicted to porn at historically unprecedented rates. Why? Many reasons, I'm sure. One reason is the sheer accessibility of porn through the web. We haven't seen the full assault of the outcomes this will produce in our society.[xxiv]

But already we are seeing that about one in five children ages 12 and 13 years old think there is nothing wrong with porn. Studies show that many in the younger generation believe porn is more immoral than failing to recycle. That's right: throwing your plastic fork in the trash can is MORE immoral than watching porn.

Here's the deal: **your children will – at some point - be exposed to porn.** The question is, for we who are parents, 'what can we do to help prepare them for and prevent them from getting addicted to porn?'

I've helped raise three children. I know this struggle well and deeply. I am going to give you a few suggestions that may help you in your quest to keep your kid and our world free of porn.

1. **Don't over react.** When you discover that your child has been or is actively viewing porn, take a few minutes and absorb the reality. You will, no doubt, experience a wide range of powerful emotions. I know my wife and I did.

Our oldest son was introduced to porn at the age of ten. He was given pictures by a classmate during school. We freaked out and that didn't help. Remember, your child probably stumbled into this or was introduced to it through no fault of his/her own.

Viewing porn has likely caused emotions to stir and desires to fire inside of them that they are unable to process. In other words, they are already dazed and confused from the experience. The last thing they need is a parental unit to double down on the reaction and drive them into a state of panic or emotional shut down.

By the way, if you have already over reacted, take heart. Many of us have and do over react. Just begin to implement some of the steps in this post and learn from others who have walked the road you now walk. Take a minute. Talk to your spouse or a close friend or family member. Develop a strategy that is *drenched in love and generosity*.

2. **Keep lines of communication open.** If we overreact, we shut them down. If we under-react, we send all sorts of nonverbal messages that produce unintended and often unhealthy consequences. So, typically, Melissa and I begin by exploring what we find, discover or has been revealed.

This commitment to exploration is a great asset in building bridges of communication and commitment. A commitment to exploring prevents false or partially true accusations and provides room for our children to develop healthy responses to situations that are beyond their reach, so to speak.

The goal is to build bridges, not erect walls. Open lines or pathways of communication are possible because of the bridges we have built and are committed to building. Communication requires engagement with our children and provides opportunities take joy in the lives our children are living. Open lines of communication mean that we ask questions - often too many in their minds - and we create space to sit and listen. Open lines of communication mean that we strive and hope to react with appropriate emotional responses.

3. **Establish fair but firm boundaries – or 'safe zones' - regarding technology.** I would suggest that you develop – with your children – some mutually agreed upon boundaries even as you reserve the right to implement one or two from on high, as it were.

Boundary development will take time, energy, grace and fortitude (remember: once you implement them, you need to abide by them), but it's well worth the investment. Here are a few suggestions for you:

    a. I repeat: No technology behind closed doors. Especially

the bedroom and bathroom. Have you been wondering why your thirteen year old spend so much time in the bath room these day?
   b. Lock social media apps at certain times during the evening. You also need to be aware of every app your child is using.
   c. Passwords must be shared with you and you are free to access the device at any time.
   d. No deleting of messages or history.
   e. _____

4. **Be honest and transparent about your own struggles and/or use of technology.** I got hooked on porn at a young age. Even today, two decades into my life free from this addiction, I have accountability software on all my screens and devices. My wife has access to everything I do and knows all the passwords I use!

When my children discovered my journey and the struggle I had/have, they became far more open to sharing their struggles and revealing their problems to both Melissa and I. When they realized that I 'play by the same rules' they play by, they became more open to the boundaries and safeguards we instituted.

5. **Know your children's friends and their friend's family!** This is crucial and often ignored. Take time to get to know your kids friends and their family. Have them over for dinner. Meet the parents at the mall for ice cream.

Whatever you do, do NOT allow your children to spend unaccountable hours in the home of people that you don't know and have no authority over. When you meet a kid, if your *spider senses* start tingling, hit the brakes – you are probably right. Have *them over* and invite them into your home a few times before allowing your son or daughter to go to their house.

This is basic parenting 101. Talk about your concerns with your child and see if they have noticed something as well. In all likely hood, they haven't. They will probably disagree with you and argue against your decision to hit the brakes. They may say mean things, intended to harm you. But you know what? One day they will no longer be a 'know it all teenager'. They will - one day - be parents themselves. *Your decisions to act in the best regard for your child today is going to help them act in the best regard for your grandchild tomorrow.* Be involved!

On a final note. Not to sound too terribly alarmist, but porn addiction is a global epidemic that is quickly approaching pandemic levels. We cannot ignore it or wish it away. The porn industry is well funded and highly connected to some of the most influential leaders in our country. While you may not be a porn addict, we are a nation of addicts.

In our home *protocol* is an agreed-upon guideline/procedure designed to protect, create space, and encourage the fullest development of the God-given treasure within our heart. The protocol – though agreed upon – is often the result of deep reflection, impassioned dialogue and a broken heart or two. *It's not a formula for they who desire the path of ease, but a pathway for we who desire life giving richness in the most meaningful realities of our life.*

I'd encourage you to utilize this information to develop a comprehensive approach and strategy related to how you want to parent against porn. While some of this information is going to necessarily overlap, I am going to share our family plan that we utilized and leaned upon often while our children were in our home!

First, let's take a look at some core values or pre-commitments regarding establishing family-wide protocol.

Core Values of Our Personal Family Protocol

1. Any protocol should come from a place of love and proactive desire. Our goal is the fullest development of our children's lives, as well as our own.

2. Common Agreements. Any protocol should be built upon some common agreements. Yes, you will have to draw a hard line in some cases, but we have found that our children can and do contribute to the development of our protocol in meaningful

ways.

3. Pathway for All. Any protocol should have the capacity to guide and serve as a pathway for the entire family – not just the children.

The values expressed above serve as a foundation or soil, if you will, in which our protective measures may grow and flourish. Each value expresses the significance of everyone's sense of personhood, plac'dness and purpose.

Our Family Porn Prevention Protocol

Mutual Commitment/Affirmation: We agree and will try to abide by the following protocol in our home and our life away from home. When we do not abide by these agreements, we will honestly confess our failure and or shortcomings. We will trust in one another's response and reaffirm our desire to move toward wholeness as we recommit ourselves to protecting the treasure of our heart!

1. All technology will utilize accountability, reporting or web block software.
2. No phones, tablets or personal electronic devices of any kind are EVER allowed in the bathroom (trust us on this one).
3. No phones, tablets or computers in bedrooms overnight.
4. Children may, at any time, hold parents accountable to all agreed upon protocol established above – without question.
5. Any protocol may be changed or altered if an agreement can be reached. Remember, mom's vote counts as 2 to our 1.

As parents of three young people now in the teen years of life, we know that any boundary or protocol can be easily overcome and bypassed. So, our number one protocol is simply this:

We are committed to building bridges toward you each other. Bridges that provide avenues where we might grow and flourish – both today and tomorrow!

Remember, our goal is to build bridges, not erect walls. Any protocol is possible because of the bridges we have built and are committed to building. This particular protocol requires engagement with our children and provides opportunities take joy in the lives our children are living.

It *means that we ask questions – often too many in their minds – and we create space to sit and listen. It means we strive to react with appropriate emotional responses.*

If we overreact, we shut them down. If we under-react, we send all sorts of nonverbal messages that produce unintended and often unhealthy consequences. So, typically, we begin by exploring what we find, discover or is revealed. This commitment to exploration is a great asset in building bridges of communication and commitment. A commitment to exploring prevents false or partially true accusations and provides room for our children to develop healthy responses to situations that are beyond their reach, so to speak.

Yeah, we know. It's not rocket science. To many it's too little, to some, it's too much. Your protocol will, no doubt, flesh out somewhat differently than ours. It is our hope, however, that this post will serve to encourage you along these lines.

Perhaps knowing others have faced and continue to face the challenges of guiding, guarding and growing will encourage you; give you hope. Providing the confidence you need to step forward and parent your family in ways that protect and preserve the God-given treasures of their heart!

Before we jump into some other strategies for personal freedom, let's turn our attention – briefly – to the world of social media,

A Father's Confession: How Instagram Made Me Feel Like a Fool

I blew it, I confess.

I've never truly monitored Instagram the way it ought to be

monitored.

Why?

Because the social media app comes with a "T" rating, which means – ostensibly – that it's a #Pornfree app. However, this couldn't be further from the truth.

Instagram is certainly not #pornfree. The opposite, in fact is true! Instagram is a significant producer and/or provider of #freeporn.

What makes this deceptive rating even worse it that Instagram has become one of the most popular social media app among children between the ages of eight and twelve.

Yes, you read that right. But, in case you're slow – like I have been over the past five to seven years – let me translate it for you:

Instagram is providing free, easily accessible, deceptively packaged, and impossible-to-ignore pornographic images and videos to our eight year old children.

And you've been waiting until they are twelve to talk to them about sex.

My confession: I had no idea Instagram provided such filth.

I have both a personal and nonprofit account for MenAgainstPorn.

I know, and have known, for some time, that Instagram features models half-dressed bikini clad models looking longingly into the camera.

I've known that broken hearts like the Kardashian daughters have modeled sexual objectification and subjugation for years. They have, almost single-handedly, created a culture of young girls who have long modified 'selfies' to feature breasts and butts designed to grab the attention of horny boys and men everywhere.

I've have known that fitness models aggressively use this tool to sell their product with images displaying the bodies we all wish to obtain. The aggressive marketing typically features the 'sexy' muscles that are sure to draw a crowd.

What I've never realized it that, behind its happy selfie-life is the best life exterior, Instagram is rotten to the core.

Toxic from the inside out.

Indeed. Instagram has made me feel like a fool. But I am a fool no longer.

I recently read an article by Protect young Minds.

The article exposes the dark side of the Instagram app by revealing that pornographic images and videos are surreptitiously located within the world of instaposts!

I couldn't believe it. So, I fact-checked them.

Guess what?

They're right. Spot on with NO exaggeration.

I began by simply scrolling down my search window (something every one of our kids do all the time!).

I then clicked on a fairly mild pic of a pretty girl in a bikini.

It was a one-of-three images format. I think they call this the 'magazine.'

The images got progressively more degrading and sexually suggestive. I then checked out 'followers' and found a host of accounts that provide sex scenes that leave nothing to the imagination.

This process took a total of about five minutes.

Here's the deal: I come out of a porn addiction.

I've fought hard for my freedom and maintained my freedom (by the grace of God) for twenty years.

Yet, even at that, I was tempted to look for more and find more sexually explicit material – all provided on a social media app that bills itself as acceptable for teens.

This is an outrage.

If I slipped into something like this ten years ago, who knows where it would have taken me. What do you think the result will be when your honestly curious and wonderfully energetic eight year old son does the same?

Instagram, you and the executives who stir the waters of this cesspool you invite us all to swim in, should be ashamed.

I confess: I've been a fool. But I will be a fool no longer.

Social Media and Secret Shame

"I have terrible trust issues. Ever since middle school and everybody got their phones. I don't feel like I can trust anyone." ~Carrie, 15 year-old teen from Boca Raton, FL.

I recently picked up an important book, from which I extracted the quote above. It's called, *American Girls: Social Media and the Secret Lives of Teenagers,* by Nancy Jo Sales. Carrie, and the host of teenaged girls studied in this groundbreaking book, goes on to describe the world of *Finstas*.

Finstas are fake Instagram accounts that middle school aged and younger children create to keep them hidden from their parents. Do you know if your child has a *Finsta?*

I discovered the *Finsta* about two years ago, while researching the topic of porn and teens. I'd encourage you to do the same, particularly if you have preteen or teenage daughters in your home (*Finstas* seem to be populated primarily by girls).

Welcome to the world of your children. Social Media apps dominate and dictate their external and – we are finding – their internal environment.

Yes.

Social Media is leading to increased stress and anxiety.

Social Media is also leading to isolation and a feeling of disconnectedness among teens (adults as well).

This stress, anxiety, and disconnect seems to result in a spike in divisiveness and conflict among teenagers, especially girls.

As Dara, another one of the students Sales spends time with, remarks:

> *"I feel like saying things on social media is so much easier. But if you say something on Facebook, it hurts the same amount as if the person said it to your face;* **but that person doesn't think about it because they're just typing it on a computer."**

Sales makes the argument, quite persuasively, that the Technology industry is, perhaps unwittingly, in bed with the Porn industry. The Porn industry, of course, confesses openly that without technology their outreach and revenue would be nearly non-existent.

One might even dub the internet **Porn's Super Highway**. Note just a few statistics from studies gathered between 2014 and 2015:

- 1 in 5 Mobile searches are for Porn. (Covenant Eyes, Porn Stats Annual Report 2015).
- **Mobile porn is expected to reach $2.8 billion by 2015.** I'm not sure what the revenue is this year.

- 37% of 3 and 4 year olds use their parent's tablets and smartphones as do 87% of 5 to 7 year olds. (http://www.familysafemedia.com/pornography_statistics.html - accessed June 6, 2014).
- A third of 11 to 14 year olds have watched porn on a mobile device. Jonathan Blake, "Mobile porn access 'damaging' children and teenagers," BBC Newsbeat, 2/11/14, at http://www.bbc.co.uk/newsbeat/26122390

Sales then goes on to make the claim that Silicon Valley, which is the epicenter of technological invention, *is infected with a frat-boy, porn-saturated culture at every level.* As such, the hub of our technological development is infused with porn-industry ideology. If she's correct, and she cites an array of data to substantiate her claim, then the outcomes of Silicon Valley's inventions should concern every one of us!

Studies reveal that many *teenagers spend up to 9 hours a day on social media apps.* Each app is littered with images that *pornify* women and distort one's image of womanhood. Porn, at every level, objectifies women. As such, pornography creates a perspective among our teenage boys and girls that alters how they relate to one another.

What can be done?

I know that Social Media is here to stay.

So do you.

But, what can we do, as parents, to help free our children (especially our daughters) from the stress and anxiety these apps seem to create?

Let me offer a few pieces of advice:

1. **Model healthy behavior as it relates to smartphone use.** One way to do this is to wait until your children are thirteen to fifteen years of age before you allow them to 'own' a smartphone or tablet. This is going to be tough. There's nothing magical about

the ages I'm proposing, but I can tell you that eight-years-old is too young and some children have access to them at two or three years old.

2. **Monitor the devices and screens in your home.** Talk openly about your child's smart phone usage and have access to all their apps, accounts, passwords, etc. Generally, we tend to monitor every part of our children's lives until it comes to this most important part. You don't have to be a dictator. Discuss what you expect and want to see happen and get their input.

3. **Minimize screen/phone input and exposure!** Challenge your child (and do this with them) to relinquish their phones for a week. Studies reveal the quite significant, immediate, and positive effects of challenges like this.

In my hometown, a teacher challenges her class, yearly, to go without smartphones for a week. The results are encouraging, as this YouTube (https://youtu.be/qrmZ6jLTezk) clip reveals.

A larger study, conducted at UCLA in 2014 found that sixth-graders who went just five days without a smartphone, television, or other screens were significantly better at reading human emotions in face-to-face communication than sixth graders from the same school who continued using their electronic devices (American Girls, page 136).

In some ways, it's not really *what* your child is doing on their phone as much as it is *that* they are on their phones too much.

A Quick Comment on Gaming and Porn

A few years ago, Singapore based game publisher, IGG, saw their annual revenue jump over 200%. Their popular Castle Clash accounted for nearly 80% of the jump. What you may not realize it that kids who play this game are given access to thousands of other games, for free.

Dozens, possibly hundreds, maybe thousands (the number is too high to count), of those other games are explicitly pornographic.

All of the games are free.

All of the games are easy to download and disguise.

Parents never have to know.

The global gaming industry is one that's been teen-friendly (as a distributor of porn and exploiter of our children) for decades.

IGG-games is no exception.

In fact, parents, you need to know that IGG offers porn to your 'gaming-child' for free.

Yes, they offer games like Honey Select free-of-charge, to children of ANY age.

Others titles (again free) in their library?
- Porno Studio Tycoon
- Drunken Robot Pornography
- Bad Ass Babes
- Beauty Bounce
- Beach Life: Virtual Resort: Spring Break
- Detective Masochist (Yes, you read it right)
- Nefarious (as sickening as it is, an "adult" edition featuring anime characters designed to look like preteens)

Some of the games even offer dating advice to your six year old.

And all of it's free.

By the time you get around to reading this much is likely to have changed. Hopefully this information will encourage you to take nothing for granted when it comes to your child and his or her access to social media!

6 PRACTICING RHYTHMS OF GRACE

EXPERIENTIAL PRACTICES AS A RELIABLE PATHWAY TOWARD OUR FREEDOM.

When I was a boy, my father kept a garden. Each spring he would begin preparing the land, planting the seed, nurturing the soil, etc. By mid-June, continuing through late August, we would harvest a great variety of vegetables.

If it grew in dirt, my dad planted it. While the garden was not too terribly large, I was not fond of the work it required! In my mind the garden may as well have been a mile long and a mile wide. As a young and active boy I would rather have spent my summer days doing anything other than weeding and tilling the soil.

I disliked the hard work and effort, yet I enjoyed the rewards of my labor. My favorite vegetables are tomatoes, okra, peanuts, corn, and the variety of melons we planted each year.

The fruit of my labor redeemed the sweat of my brow. I also learned a few lessons through my *gardening experience.* The lessons I learned have continued to shape me well into my adult years and have been pivotal for my journey out of porn addiction.

The Garden of Grace-Filled, Life-Giving Rhythms

The top three lessons I learned while gardening are listed below:

1. If you plant in and care for healthy soil, your reward will be great indeed.

2. You must pay attention and give energy to the garden daily. If you miss a few days, the weeds come roaring in, and the bugs come buzzing back.

3. You reap what you sow. Plant a squash seed and squash grows. Plant a seed for beans and you get beans. We never, not once,

reaped a melon from a bean seed. This lesson is of particular interest for those who long to live a porn-free life!

I have found these three lessons extend well beyond gardening. They provide insight into the importance of cultivating the meaningful roles and relationships in which we find ourselves on a daily basis.

Consider, for example, the meaningful role and relationship of marriage and family.

Melissa and I have been married since 1995. We have much to celebrate. Our marriage is not perfect. But, our marriage is strong. Ours is a union full of spiritual, physical, sexual, and emotional intimacy. This intimacy is the soil of our marriage, cultivated day in and day out. An intimacy we forge in the intricacies and challenges of raising kids, battling sickness, and paying the bills. Those routine and regular moments that shape and define us.

Put more simply: we work hard at our love. It never has - not even for one moment - just happened. We have battled through personal addictions and deeply rooted, family-of-origin issues (yeah, you know what I'm talking about). We have wrestled through long nights of intense care over sick babies who refused to sleep, babies whose lone comfort seemed to derive from parental fatigue.

We have wrangled through ministry years that were bleak and seasons when our sense of *identity and calling* were criticized and questioned. We muddled our way through a particularly difficult season of lymphoma. A season during which our children - then ages five, seven, and nine - watched as a wonderfully strong and vibrant mother dwindled into a weakened chemo-ridden version of the mom they once knew.

Twenty plus years of wrestling, wrangling, and muddling our way through life into a wonderful and hard-won intimacy. Far from perfect, yet not so far from fulfilling. We have three beautiful teenage children who offer themselves and their gifting to the world in considerable ways. We are far from the finish line, but we enjoy over twenty years of cultivating life in the routine moments and daily distresses.

The fruit of our life is filled already with *sink-your-teeth-into* flavor: three beautiful children, dozens - if not hundreds - of meaningful relationships, and a marital union that produces fruit with each passing day.

Where we are **now** is because of what we did **then**!

In other words, the decisions we made in our past have led us to the joys we celebrate in our present. We have tended the soil and cared for its health. We have worked on - **daily** - the *love of us*. In moments when we have sown love, we have reaped wonder.

Generally speaking, we reap the harvest we sow. As such, it's no surprise to me that we are a culture consumed by and conformed to pornography addiction. Put differently: when the soil of our culture nurtures the plant of pornography, the fruit is always something akin to **Fifty Shades of Grey.**

It's no surprise to me. Nor should it be to you. Our decisions have led us here. The seed we have sown is the fruit we now reap.

My answer to the *what then* question is captured in the quote by Thomas Chalmers, taken from a sermon that's decades old:

> **"The only way to dispossess the heart of an old affection is by the expulsive power of a new affection."**

We might focus on the development of virtues and disciplines that will cultivate fertile soil in our lives and community. Soil in which the life-giving rhythms of love, intimacy, and sexual desire might flourish and choke out the teeming waters of conflict, control, and sexual subjugation - drowning one and all.

We begin with rhythms that we can practice in the 'daily grind.' It's here, in our walkabout world, where porn's influence is notably felt. Therefore, it's logical to learn how to orient ourselves to the world in a way that will diminish porn's pull and accentuate love's call!

Granular Rhythms of Grace: Practicing and Celebrating the Presence of Christ in our midst

Over the past ten years I have experimented with what I call the ***granular rhythms of grace***. These rhythms are ones that awaken me to the transcendent presence of God and lead me to anticipate His *in-breaking* all around.

Perhaps some definitions will help:

Granular – made of or appearing to be made of small pieces, particles, or granules. Granular, then, means the ordinary moments of our life. Those small and seemingly insignificant interactions, experiences, and projects that shape reality.

Moments such as emails, phone calls, doing the laundry, changing the diapers, writing that paper, holding that meeting, mowing the lawn, etc.

Rhythms – strong, regular, and repeated pattern of movements. The term rhythms serves as a reminder that much of life is the experience of repeated patterns of behavior.

For example, brushing teeth, eating, sleeping, etc. Our world – though often chaotic and fast-paced – is lived within the context of overarching rhythms that govern our relationships and interactions.

Grace – God in action on our behalf. I know that's probably not the typical definition of grace, yet I believe it captures what the Scriptures teach.

The practice of rhythms of grace, then, is the practice of rhythms – in the midst of daily life – that remind one that God is – even in the thickest, darkest, and most mundane moments of life – in action on one's behalf.

These granular rhythms of grace are simple, but they embody a power that can shape the soul. Their power is based upon practicing them as repeatable patterns in the daily grind of life.

In other words, as we work on them they work on us!

Over time and by grace an awareness of God in the grind will shape us to expect Him to reveal His glory! These rhythms, and a host of others like them, have helped shape - in me - a way of life that's sacred, soul-full, and ultimately satisfying.

Granular Rhythms That Reinforce God's Presence Among Us

1. **Be in the Moment and Be Where You Are!** We live in a *presently-absent* world. We are often trying to do more than one thing at a time and are rarely focused in on only one person at a time. Such frenetic, soul-sucking tendencies rob us of the beauty of the moment and the people with us!

    One of my primary granular rhythms of grace is to settle into the moments and people I am with in this life. God has peeled back the sky many times during moments when I have been fully attentive to and aware of each moment I am in and the people I am with!

2. **Pause Regularly and Behold Beauty Often!** Most of us overload our calendars. We are simply too busy: rushing from one thing or event to the next thing or event at a break-neck pace.

    I'm not saying you need to stop all you are doing, but I would encourage you to schedule – within even your busiest days – one or two 10 - 15 minute renewal pauses. Take some time and read the scriptures, pray, call a loved one, or go out and stare into the sky.

    I find that when I plan to behold the beauty God has provided all around me, I am more open to His presence with me and others He places in my midst.

3. **Seek Moments When You Can Put Others First!** If our current imaginary is shaped by self-absorption, self-sufficiency, and self-centeredness, then this rhythm is essential if we hope for a paradigm shift. It's also rewarding, most of the time.

   Begin by simply engaging your waiter or waitress in meaningful conversation when you are eating your lunch. Or try not to honk your horn so much (which, by the way, serves as a default practice that reinforces the current soul-sucking imaginary). Maybe you could hold the door for someone who has their hands full. Buy doughnuts for your garbage collector.

   You get the idea. **Just get out of your head and into someone else's heart.**

4. **Arrest Negative, Critical Thoughts!** One of the most notable outcomes of our current imaginary is our penchant to choose "fight or flight" as our dominant means of social engagement.

   This fight or flight mentality is nurtured in the self-absorbed, self-sufficient, and self-centered imaginary. Therefore, our first response to something that is happening to us or around us is, in all likelihood, pretty messed up. So, don't entertain it. Arrest it and sever the root.

   Then replace it with generous thoughts and express them in kind words. This one is difficult to practice but probably the most necessary one when it comes to people within our immediate family and friends. I can draw a pretty straight line from conflict between people to critical thoughts nurtured within people.

5. **Practice Screen-Free Zones!** I am not an advocate of living a screen-free life. I love my screens and receive much joy from watching them and utilizing them for good in this world (yes, that's possible). But, I am a proponent of strategic screen-free zones.

   In other words, you might leave your phone at the office when you go grab a bite to eat. An important one, in my life, is to turn off my screens an hour or two before I go to bed at night. I also try to enjoy my morning before I grab my technology. I know that once I grab my phone or go to my computer, I will not soon leave it/them behind.

The Rhythms of Self-Suspicion and Blessing

It takes courage to let go of things you hold firmly and test them in the presence of God. It takes courage to say to God, as David did, "test me and see if there is any unclean way in me."

In short, it takes courage to practice the **Rhythm of Self-Suspicion.**

This ancient rhythm – always practiced for the good of one's soul and social imaginary – takes courage at the highest level because the practice scrutinizes our unwritten rules and hidden regulations that govern motives. We may find that – through the practice of Self-Suspicion - we are wrong.

God may call us to drop our "precious" ideas, convictions, and commitments and seek after Him and His good instead.

Ruth Halcy Barton, of the Transforming Center, when teaching on Examen (an ancient discipline or rhythm of reflection), reminds us of the type of courage required to practice the Rhythm of Self-Suspicion when she writes,

> *It takes courage to invite God to search and know us at the deepest levels of our being, allowing him to show us the difference between the driven-ness of the false self and the deeper calling to lead from our authentic self in God. There is an elemental chaos that gets stirred up when we have been in God's presence enough that all pretense and performance and every other thing that has bolstered our sense of self begins to fall away.*[xxv]

We routinely pass such judgments – either unspoken or spoken – throughout the course of our week. With each opinion, decision, or pivotal moment we face, we have a choice between "driven-ness" or a "deeper calling."

Cultivating the 'deeper calling' response, however, takes practice: the practice of self-Suspicion. The practice that scrutinizes motives, and the unwritten rules that govern real-time behavior.

Having prepared us with granular rhythms of grace that more generally orient us toward God's presence, we next consider two specific rhythms of Self-Suspicion and Blessing that serve to reshape the ongoing narrative of our heart.

The reshaping of our heart – away from our distorted perceptions and toward love and others with whom we are called to share love – are the foundation stones of a porn-free life. They provide the footing needed to begin to believe that we are capable of such a life and that such a life comes with its own great, lasting, and transformational reward.

Self-Suspicion, Certainty, and the Freedom to Be True

I recall one moment in my life – years ago – in which I was certain, had a sense of clarity, and was rock-solid in my commitment regarding an important decision I needed to make. Trusting that my sense of certainty, clarity, and commitment were unwavering, I sensed that they sounded a *clarion call* to act swiftly.

As such I made a decision that – though likely the right decision – brought harm to several individuals, one family in particular, and many within the congregation – all because the three realities framed a false notion that I must act fast, with force, and finalize the decision.

Reflecting back on that moment, if I had practiced the Rhythm of Self-Suspicion in that situation, I believe I would have made the same decision, but I would have implemented the decision in an entirely different and, frankly, more affirming manner.

Why didn't I do so?

To be blunt: I lacked the courage to scrutinize my motives and thoroughly test the unwritten rules that were governing my behavior. I knew – intuitively – that if I had examined my motives, I might have been persuaded to change or reconsider my decision. I might, in short, have been compelled to let go of some assumptions I held dear.

We need to carve out ten – twelve minutes within the week to establish this as a routine and meaningful practice. The practice, like all practices that provide space for soul-transformation, is a combination of reflection and action.

Remember, just as in muscle memory, it will take about 3,000 repetitions for a practice to become a habit. In other words, this is a life-long journey, not simply a check-the-box accomplishment.

A Six-Step Rhythm of the Practice of Self-Suspicion

1. **Clear the Clutter.**

Imagining your roles and specific experiences, take a moment and reflect on the following questions designed to help you clear out the clutter and bring Christ-centered clarity:

Do I have all the information regarding this specific moment or situation?

Have I considered all the ramifications of the actions I will take?

Are there any unhealthy attachments related to ego, position, selfish desires, etc., that are clouding my judgment?

2. **Center Your Soul on Christ.**

In this step, simply bring the reflections and conclusions from step one and offer them to Christ. Read and reflect on a specific bible verse and ask God's Spirit to reveal His truth through

His word. Sit quietly in this place and listen to the Lord's voice (You may want to jot down the leadings you receive).

3. **Climb into a Place of Surrender to Christ.**

After hearing from the Lord, you may realize that you need to make some personal, heart-level adjustments. He may reveal some attachments that are continuing to clutter and confound a biblical and restorative resolution.

A verse of scripture I find helpful for this step is Psalm 131:1- 2:

Lord, my heart is not proud; my eyes are not haughty. I don't concern myself with matters too great or too awesome for me to grasp. Instead, I have calmed and quieted myself, like a weaned child who no longer cries for its mother's milk. Yes, like a weaned child is my soul within me.

To rest in the lap of the Lord and be content in His provision is the ultimate goal of this particular rhythm.

4. **Pray to be Released from Your Attachments.**

In my current leadership position, I pastor a local congregation. While I am the Senior Pastor, I've always sought to participate in and practice "shared leadership."

This means that our leadership team strives to make shared decisions that are birthed from a healthy process of discernment.

During our years together, we've discovered a prayer[xxvi] that we've learned to pray with consistency. It's a prayer that replaces, over time, our personal attachments as we learn to trust in the leading of the Lord. This prayer is one you might consider praying in this step:

> **"Lord, I want your will. Nothing more, nothing less, nothing else. Amen!"**

5. **Celebrate the Outcome by Calling on an Objective Friend to Pray with and Guide You.**

We are designed to experience meaningful and life-giving community. Therefore, as you discover the Lord's leading, I'd encourage you to celebrate that leading with a trusted friend even as you ask him or her to be a sounding board and a prayer partner in your discovery.

It's important that we develop a way to test our inclinations and submit to the input of others, whom we trust, and who provide objective voices in regard to the specific situation or opportunity.

6. Proceed to Implement the Outcome He is Inviting You to Pursue.

As we come to a place of contentment and trust in the Lord's leading, we must take the step of acting on that leading. Simply put, do what you believe the Lord is calling you to do. Trust that He is leading and try to be open to His presence as you go.

As I said, this is just a practice. I'm not offering some magic bullet here. In fact, what I'm inviting you to is counter-cultural on nearly every level.

The Granular Rhythm of Blessing

"Blessing is not only the place from which we've come; it's the place toward which we are headed. Blessing is nothing less than the bookend of life. The power of a public, verbal, and embodied blessing breaks open the sacred beauty of the soul."

Light is a collection of a multitude of colors: green, blue, orange, red, indigo, yellow, and violet.

In order to see the rainbow of colors contained within a ray of light, one needs a prism.

A prism breaks open the light so that one can behold the beauty inside.[xxvii]

A public, verbal, and embodied (or physical) blessing breaks open the sacred beauty of one's soul by imparting life-giving rhythms of personhood, plac'dness, and purpose!

Rainbows happen when light refracts, at the appropriate angle, through rain drops. We behold the beauty of broken light when a rainbow appears on the horizon.

The beauty is so wonderfully astounding that we literally pause what we're doing to behold, but for a moment, the beauty that's on full display.

The commingling of rain with light in the atmosphere creates an environment in which beauty becomes the norm, washing away the dreary and the drab. It holds our attention just long enough for us to listen to the roar of our heart - the yearning for more - exclaimed deep within the soul.

As a prism breaks open light, so a blessing breaks open the human heart.

Yes, a public, verbal, and embodied blessing, generously given, will produce an outcome that will cause us to stop and beg for more.

For a soul and society bent on cursing, the power of blessing offers an untapped reservoir of nourishment!

It's a reservoir from which we not only drink, but one from which we're also invited and encouraged to share!

Why is there such power in blessing?

Because blessing is a creational gift of God which originally bestowed His good upon the world. Life begins in blessing. We also noted that life ends in blessing.

Indeed, blessing stands as the bookend of life. Eternity is, at the least, an experience of unending blessing.

As Tolkien once penned,

"We all long for Eden, and we are constantly glimpsing it: our whole nature at its best and least corrupted, its gentlest and most human, is still soaked with the sense of exile."

Having experienced blessing, in and through primordial grace, we now long for it in the midst of the perpetual grind.

And, though these eternal dynamics are always in play when a blessing is in motion, the blessing itself – public, verbal, and embodied – contains three heart-pumping distinctives that, when activated, bring delight to one's life!

I'm now going to share a few specific spiritual disciplines/rhythms I have found helpful in my journey.

I invite you to consider exploring and incorporating these rhythms as regular stops on your journey out of porn addiction.

1. **The Rhythm of Examen and Confession.** You must confess your addiction to your loved one(s). Confession is not an apology. In today's climate where we say ***sorry*** for everything and take responsibility for nothing - apologies are cancerous.

    Confession should be full and complete. Anything less will wreck the healing process and cause further damage to yourself and those you love. You may begin by confessing to yourself. A personal acknowledgement that you are in too deep is a great place to start.

    Then, find a trusted friend, one who will not judge you, but who will encourage you toward wholeness. At some point, when it's time, you will need to confess to your loved one(s) whom you have harmed. This confession will require care and support, but it is vital if you are to tend healthy soil!

    I'd encourage you to begin your discovery of confession by practicing an ancient and powerful spiritual rhythm called Examen.

While there are many adaptations of this available through a variety of means, I am going to include one that I use on a regular basis:

Practicing a Review of the Day (Examen)*
My prayer is that light will flood your hearts . . . Ephesians 1:18

Become aware of God's presence. Reflect on the presence of God in your midst throughout your day (Psalm 139).

Review with gratitude. Gratitude is the foundation of our relationship with God. Walk through your day in the presence of God and note its joys and delights.
- For what moment today am I most or least grateful?
- What were today's high and low points?
- What was it today that was most life-giving or draining?
- When today did I have the greatest/least sense of belonging to myself, others, and God?
- When did I sense connection/disconnection with God?
- When did I give and receive the most/least love today?
- When was I the most happy or most sad today?

Choose one feature from your day and ask the Holy Spirit to lead you into confession and gratitude.
- Notice launching points for gratitude/confession.

Look toward tomorrow. Thank God for His presence with you in the past day and anticipate His presence in the day to come. Leave with Christ whatever struggles and sins presented themselves. Rest in the assurance of forgiveness.

> *In the end, the prayer of Examen is about noticing: noticing the good gifts God gives us, noticing the presence of God in our lives, and noticing the ways we fail God. When we notice, we become more conscious. When we become more conscious, we grow.* —Richard Peace

*Adapted from Ignatian Spirituality -- More than 400 years ago St. Ignatius encouraged *prayer-filled mindfulness* by proposing what has become known as the Examen.

The Rhythms of Silence and Solitude.

In moments of silence, we learn a great deal about ourselves. We become aware of how terribly noise-ridden we are as a people. We also begin to discover deep wounds that noise and chaos hide so well. Over time, silence and solitude will lead us to discover our truest selves. My journey into silence often encompasses meditation on Scripture passages and historic sayings and quotes from some of my favorite figures from history.

In silence, I learn, as the Psalmist beautifully depicts, *to rest in the arms of the Lord as a weaned child.* If you're not sure how to practice this rhythm, you may want to follow this simple guideline I find helpful:

A Beginner's Guide to Silence and Solitude

Solitude is being alone with God. It is creating space in your life whereby you are able to hear Him speak to you, to call you His beloved child! In silence and solitude we learn how to listen to the Father, Son, and Holy Spirit and hear/discern His voice in the midst of many others.

- Find a space that is free from distractions. It could be a room in your home, a patio, a favorite chair, etc. It could also be a spot by the river or a favorite space on the beach (turn off all "outside" interference, i.e., your smart phone, computer, laptops, etc.).

- Relax! Most of us are new to solitude and silence, so the practice may be somewhat daunting. Enjoy the time and receive the moments Christ grants. If you can only practice for a few minutes, before being filled with distractions – take note of that and enjoy God's revelation of how truly full your life has become.

- Consider writing down a favorite Bible passage, quote, or prayer to reflect on during your time of solitude (this is not necessary, but it may be helpful for those who are not accustomed to silence and solitude). A favorite passage may help you maintain focus and a listening posture before the Lord.

- When you have completed your time of solitude, I invite you to reflect with someone about your experience of this practice. Remember, we are practicing together this week, so there are others who would love to hear about your victories as well as struggles.

It is possible to have silence, to be still, and to know that the Lord is God (**Ps. 46: 10**), and to set the Lord before our minds with sufficient intensity and duration that we stay centered upon him – our hearts fixed, established in trust (**Ps. 112: 7– 8**) – even when back in the office, shop, or home.

The Sabbath Rhythm.

Establishing a twenty-four-hour period of rest is a rejuvenating rhythm that will restore interior graces necessary for living a flourishing and fulfilling life. I often reflect back on my gardening experience when I consider Sabbath rest. My father would give different areas of soil a rest from time to time - allowing the nutrients to reform and revitalize the earth. We are similarly like the soil: we need moments of rest so that we might be revitalized and rejuvenated for the journey yet to come.

The Rhythm of Honesty.

Honesty may be the most vital rhythm of all. You must practice honesty at every level and in all relationships. Honesty commences when you cease the ***self-lie*** that enables your distortion in the first place. The Psalmist reminds us that the one who will dwell on the Lord's holy hill is "***the one who speaks truth in his heart.***"

Interior truth is where all truth must begin.

The rhythm of honesty is vastly important. As a man recovering from addiction, I've found that I'm prone to accept lies and perpetuate them. Such a proclivity has caused me to drill down to the granular realities (bills, work, fatigue, etc.) that cause this proclivity.

I recently read a wonderful article that describes the purpose of spiritual disciplines and rhythms in an enticing way:

> *The (spiritual) disciplines are practices of resistance against the old habits that we repent of* **and** *they strategically cultivate new habits. They are the rhythms of everyday discipleship.* **The goal is not to just kill the weeds of vice but to cultivate a garden of Christ-like virtues.**[xxviii]

The Zombie Apocalypse is upon us.

It remains in our hands how widespread the chaos will become!

7 PATHWAYS OF AND PILLARS IN OUR JOURNEY OF PERSONAL FREEDOM

DISCOVERING FOUR REPEATABLE PILLARS OF FREEDOM AND RESTORATION

Looking back on my journey out of porn and into my truest self, I have come to see that it has been marked by seasons of screaming my way through the pain the porn produced in the hope of easing my way into the joy freedom provides.

The last portion of that statement is important for those who desire to be free from porn. It's important to know that there is a palpable ease into freedom which provides joy.

Yes!

The best and truest self is the one who lives at ease in the celebration of joy.
You can be this person. You can taste this joy.

The taste of joy, the ease of freedom, does not manifest itself at the expense of pain. Rather, the taste of joy and the ease of freedom are provided by the pathway of pain. That's why I often say I spent years of my life screaming my way into freedom. I believe my experience is normative, to a degree.

I believe, at least, that none of us will ever enjoy the ease of freedom and the fruit of joy if we aren't willing and ready - really vulnerable enough - to experience the pain and endure the need to scream.

I am going to share four personal pillars of freedom that I continue to return to on a weekly, sometimes daily, basis. The screaming is - at least for now - over.

The freedom? That's lasting!

I hope this provides a pathway for those who long to be free!

Four Repeatable and Personal Pillars of Freedom

1. Contemplation: Examining Thought Behavior!

This constitutes a portion of the screaming that must be endured. Any freedom begins with a willingness to admit one's current bondage and then examine the thought behaviors that nurture the addiction. I am suggesting that we have certain *thought behaviors* or patterns that lead us toward addiction and nurture the soil in which addiction grows.

For example, let's say my wife refuses to be intimate with me. I likely have a *thought behavior* that processes that rejection. I probably tell myself something like, "she just doesn't care about me," or "she is so selfish," or "how am I supposed to stay faithful when she refuses me?" These are all thought behaviors or patterns that are simply not connected with reality.

Seriously, she may actually have a headache. Or, she may be tired from taking care of the kiddos all day long. Or, work may have been stressful, etc. Point is - there are other options for our thought patterns that do not take us down the pathway to our porn addiction!

We must examine these thought behaviors, arrest them, and then replace them with positive patterns of response!

2. Confession: Experiencing and Expressing the Pain Porn Causes!

More screaming, I know. Yet the porn addict has to look directly into the eyes of those whom his/her addiction has been brutalizing and experience the pain they feel and express sorrow over the pain the addiction is causing.

This is the most difficult step of all! If you truly want to be healed, live with hope, and experience wholeness, then this is the only option for you. If you are unable to take this step right now - don't give up on your freedom.

Pillar number four may provide the support you need for such a step. These steps are not, by the way, linear. They are often erratic, surprising, and disruptive, but rarely - if ever - are they linear and/or manageable.

3. Community: Engaging In Relationships and Resources That Offer Health, Hope, and Wholeness!

This phase endures the screaming even as it experiences the easing of pain! We all - every human on the planet - have a primordial desire to connect with others in a significant and life-giving way.

Porn addiction exploits and distorts this desire as it numbs you to the hope that you will ever experience it.

If you are active in your porn addiction, then this deep, eternal, and sacred desire has likely been numbed. You are probably the poster child of the presently-absent culture we have become! The step you must take is one of engaging in meaningful relationships with others - preferably others who can assist you on your journey toward your truest self.

I encourage you to find a friend or counselor or minister, etc., with whom you can share your story and from whom you can find strength, hope, and joy! There are numerous resources that can aid you in this respect. There are online courses/resources[xxix] to help you experience freedom as well as ongoing support groups[xxx] that focus on this particular addiction.

4. Communion: Explore the Beauty of God and the Joy of His Love For You!

I began to experience freedom from my addiction the moment I began to explore the beauty of God and the love He has for me. Over twenty years ago a counselor recommended a twelve-week study designed to explore why I struggled with porn addiction.

While I cannot locate the workbook anywhere, nor do I remember what it was called, the first pages explored two Bible verses that opened my eyes and heart to the ease of freedom and lasting joy.

In Mark 1:9 – 11 we read:

"In those days Jesus came from Nazareth of Galilee and was baptized by John in the Jordan. 10 And when he came up out of the water, immediately he saw the heavens being torn open and the Spirit descending on him like a dove. And a voice came from heaven, "You are my beloved Son; with you I am well pleased."

I was, in that moment, as Lewis might say, 'surprised by joy.' Then the author explored a section from Romans 8 which reads:

"For all who are led by the Spirit of God are sons of God. 15 For you did not receive the spirit of slavery to fall back into fear, but you have received the Spirit of adoption as sons, by whom we cry, "Abba! Father!"

I paused in my tears and thanked God for His love over me and the beauty of His love in me! It's as if God spoke directly to me on that afternoon: "I love you, Son! You are my beloved in whom I am well pleased."

Exploring the beauty of God and experiencing the love He has for you, over you, in you, and through you is the way to replace the thought behaviors that drive you to porn.

In this way, you see, the pillars are actually more like a process.

The only way to Examine, Experience, and Engage the first three is to EXPLORE the beauty of God.

We now move from some personal pillars to how we can experience these within an ongoing community or accountability group.

8 Pathways to Freedom Within a Community of the Faithful

Discovering an Ongoing Process that Invites Community and Encourages Commitment.

Catholic theologian, Christopher West, in his excellent book *Fill These Hearts*, suggests all of our desires have a trajectory. They are, in other words, heading in some direction. As we bring our journey to a close, I'd like to pull all the pieces together and offer a way you might intentionally direct your desires toward Christ, who is our end.

I call it stealing West's terminology, **Life in 3D**:

- Exploring Desires.
- Directing them toward God.
- Discerning His will in an ongoing way.

This pathway requires community and commitment. It's a pathway that I believe is essential for one's journey into freedom.

I spent years searching for a way to partner with others struggling with addiction. I've been in and out of accountability groups, support groups, and recovery groups.

I've never experienced one that brings all the vital combinations of victory together and encourages one to discover and explore them with a group of authentic and like-minded companions.

It's my hope that "Life in 3D" Groups can be that very thing! This is something you can start right in your church and implement alongside of ongoing small groups or is something you can launch in the privacy of your home, family, neighborhood, etc.

It's a group that's open to all ages and all struggles, and one whose identity is not defined by addiction but by destination. That's an important distinction that too few make.

I am going to propose a base template to use, but the hard work of seeing it happen is up to you, and your willingness to come clean, and your desire to live a porn-free life!

Life In 3d: A Pathway To Freedom Within A Community Of The Faithful!!

3 Core Commitments/Objectives and Desires of a 3D Group!

1. Participating in a community in which you can safely and authentically explore the hidden or ignored desires of your heart.

2. Participating in a community in which your desires can be carefully, biblically, and lovingly re-directed toward God and His good in your life and the world around you.

3. Participating in a community in which you grow as a disciple or apprentice of Jesus who is able and open to discerning His will in the nooks and crannies of daily living.

The Weekly Gathering

Collecting and Connecting
- Life in 3D groups begin by simply connecting with one another. Depending upon the time of day when you meet, someone may want to bring some refreshments. Spend about 10 minutes 'breaking bread' together and catching up on life.

Hearing/Listening
- Begin with a moment (between 2 and 5 minutes) of silence. Silence is a way to create space in which we can hear from the Lord and each other as we gather.

Sharing
- Facilitator for the meeting begins and takes 5 – 7 minutes to share from his life around the following questions:

- Tell us the closest you have come to acting on an unwanted thought or behavior pattern since the last meeting what you did about it.
- Can you identify the actual trigger or the 'root' cause?
- Do you have a replacement and restoration strategy to lean on in this moment?
- Or, can you avoid the trigger or put safeguards in your life that will hold you when they fire?
- Tell us one or two affirmations about God. Tell us one or two affirmations about yourself
- In one or two words, state how you are feeling emotionally right now.

Once finished the person to his right offers a prayer for the one who shared. The group then rests in 60 seconds of silence before continuing.

Once finished, the person to his right offers a prayer for the one who shared. The group then rests in 60 seconds of silence before continuing. Repeat this process until all have shared. Remember, no one is forced to share.

Hearing/Listening
- Read the week's text contemplatively together. This means the text will be read at least three different times with silence in between each reading.

Sharing
- Spend the remaining time, as a group, sharing encouraging words to each other, specifically if you have "heard" a word from the Lord during the time of sharing. This is not a moment to offer unsolicited advice. This is simply a moment to be brothers together in the presence of Christ and support and encourage one another for the week ahead.

Serving
- We depart our company to go into our world as God's chosen agents of redemption.

- As a group, repeat the phrase:

"We depart to steward our gifts, time, talents, and treasures our King has provided in the nooks and crannies of life, as fellow travelers on a pilgrimage to our homeland."

SCRIPTURES FOR STUDY AND CONTEMPLATIVE READINGS

1. Revelation 21 – 22
2. Genesis 1 – 2 (esp. 1:26 – 31)
3. Psalm 31:51
4. Ephesians 3
5. Matthew 22:34 – 40
6. Matthew 6:19 – 22
7. Romans 12:1 - 2
8. I Corinthians 10:12 – 14
9. Ephesians 2:4 - 10
10. Matthew 18:16 – 20
11. Psalm 145
12. Ephesians 3 – 4
13. I Corinthians 13
14. Psalm 139
15. Psalm 27
16. II Peter 1

Try to follow this pattern of hearing/responding to Christ during the week.

- Read the weekly scripture passage slowly and contemplatively, several times, asking God's spirit to guide you, direct you, and enrich you as you read and listen to Him.
- Reflect on the Pathway to Freedom and assess where you are and identify where you want to be or what you perceive is your greatest need to grow in the grace of Christ this week.
- Close your time in a prayer of thanksgiving to God for his goodness, grace, and joy over you! Reach out to one of your brothers and try to connect for drinks after work, coffee before, dinner with spouses, etc.

You can live a porn-free life.

We can be the generation that ushers in the end of porn and stems the prolific tide of dehumanization it has caused!

9 REBUILDING, RESTORING AND RE-ORDERING A LIFE THAT HAS BEEN RAVAGED BY PORN

I am not a counselor, nor am I a psychiatrist.

I am not a therapist who works with those addicted to porn, or other life-draining addictions.

I am a man who has walked and continues to walk his way out of porn addiction *into the joy of and struggle for* a porn-free life.

As such, though I have read and studied dozens of books and resources related to porn addiction, nearly everything I write is birthed from my personal journey out of porn and into freedom.

Over the next few pages I am going to convey the steps my wife, family and I have taken that have led me out of porn-addiction and into my truest self.

It is, I hope, a message that provides both encouragement and equipment for those who deeply desire to have the intimacy restored in their home and to flourish together in their marriage and relationships.

I began my *marriage rebuilding process* nearly two decades ago. I have learned much through a multitude of failures and a host of victories. Each failure stemmed from an unwillingness or inability to live by established convictions related to freedom and hope.

Each victory has been birthed in the vibrant soil of these core convictions and produced an ever growing and always maturing plant deeply rooted in the goodness of life and graciousness of God.

While I do not assume my personal convictions to be normative, I suspect they may be helpful for others who hope to rebuild their marriage from the brokenness of porn. As such, this chapter will lay the framework for some core convictions that are central to one's journey into a porn-free life.

Core Convictions as We Rebuild From the Brokenness

1. **Porn is bad.** This sounds simple, but it is, unfortunately, a conviction not shared by all. Many are convinced that porn consumption and addiction poses no real threat to them or those around them. If you are going to rebuild from the brokenness, then you need to affirm this core conviction: porn steals life and, as such, brings death!

2. **Playing the victim Will Never Lead to Victory.** The choice to play the victim is an easy one for an addict to choose! And, honestly, it's partly correct. Indeed, an addict becomes a victim of his/her behavior. An addict often feels like a victim: as if there is no other choice but to consume porn and feed the sexual perversion.

Playing the victim usually means, however, that one is refusing to *own* up to one's behavior. This response is a dead end and could ultimately lead to the death of all one loves and holds dear. If you are going to rebuild from the brokenness, then this default response must stop.

3. **Self – Preservation is Not the Place to Stay.** This choice is but one step removed from the previous one. When I would enter a *self-preservation pattern*, I usually did so *before* I got caught. I would hide all the evidence, delete the history, pretend I was somewhere I wasn't, etc. Self-preservation tends to become the default

orientation of those trapped in pornography. There is a subtle danger to this response. *The practice of self-preservation leads us into patterns of isolation, deception, and mistrust.*

Once trapped in this world, we find it is very, very hard to break free. In fact, this is what I call the *compounding shame phase* of the addiction. Already shamed by the addiction, we compound our shame by entering a self - preservation pattern.

This pattern is designed to continually hide the addiction. Shame, invariably, moves one back into the response of playing the victim.

If one is to rebuild from the brokenness of porn, then openness, accountability, and confession will need to replace this common practice.

4. **Don't Swim in the Cesspool of Guilt and Shame.** Guilt and shame are not friends of the addict seeking recovery. You will, however, experience guilt when you act out. It's easy for the addict to feed this beast because he or she feels so overwhelmed by the outcomes.

I find it helpful to bring my guilt to a trusted friend and ask him to help me process where I am on this journey. Often, after a time of meaningful sharing and reflection, I am able to see how far I have come even as I realize a long journey lies yet ahead.

5. **Authenticity and Accountability Must Become the New Normal.** I am always going to be a recovering porn addict, or a porn addict in recovery. By that I mean I must always be on my guard against a relapse or falling back into the pull of porn's power.

I learned early on that ongoing and deeply authentic accountability is now the new normal. There is never a time when I will be outside of accountability. I have installed software protection on every device and screen I own. I allow my wife access to my calendar, schedule, and daily routine.

She also has all the passwords related to my accountability software. I routinely meet with men who struggle and engage in authentic relationships designed to nurture wholeness and health!

6. **Though Porn Ends in Death, it Will Not End in MY Death.** For those who are rebuilding a marriage and family from the brokenness of porn, hope is an indispensable gift of a loving God!

As long as one has breath in the lungs, there can be redemption in the heart! The more I experienced freedom from porn, the more I discovered hidden talents and gifts I did not know I had.

As you discover your own talents and gifts - hope will prevail! When feeling trapped by or pulled into the lure of porn, go out and utilize your talents and gifts in a productive and life-affirming way!

If you are a hoping to rebuild your marriage, home, and life from the brokenness of your addiction, these responses or default behaviors will never take you where you most truly long to go or allow you to be the person you most truly long to be!

These responses are, more importantly, not the only options from which the recovering porn-addict has to choose!!

Playing the victim Will Never Lead to Victory

The choice to play the victim is an easy one for an addict to choose! An addict, or someone struggling with an attraction to pornography, often feels like a victim: as if there is no other choice but to consume porn and feed the sexual perversion.

Indeed, an addict, in real ways, becomes a victim of his/her behavior.

Playing the victim usually means, however, that one is refusing to *own* up to one's behavior. This response is a dead end and could ultimately lead to the death of all one loves and holds dear.

If you are going to rebuild from the brokenness of a life ravaged by porn, then this default response must stop.

Nearly twenty years ago, I was forced to own up. My wife discovered my addiction during the moment of my consumption. This moment changed everything for me and began to usher in my long and, at times, excruciating, walk into freedom.

Looking back on that time, I can recall three building blocks that have remained firm down to this very day. If you are hoping to rebuild your life and relationships that porn is ravaging, then these building blocks might be the place where your journey begins.

Building Block #1: Confess your addiction.

This is the first step.

I began by confessing to a trusted friend who was willing to walk with me and encourage me to confess to my wife.

The pain of confession was as excruciating as the freedom from confession was liberating!

Full confession, freed from the tug of victimization, self-preservation, or blame-shifting is the most fundamental step I ever took on this journey into freedom.

Confession began (at least for me) with God. I recall vividly sensing the depth of my sin against God. After all, each image was a picture of someone's daughter, sister, mother and friend.

Like David, my heart wept before the King. God's grace allowed me to see that my sin against others - through my porn addiction - was ultimately a sin against Him.

As David cries out in Psalm 51:1 - 4, so my heart cried out before the Lord:

"Have mercy on me, God, according to your faithful love!
Wipe away my wrongdoings according to your great compassion!
Wash me completely clean of my guilt;

purify me from my sin!
Because I know my wrongdoings,
my sin is always right in front of me.
I've sinned against you—you alone.
I've committed evil in your sight.
That's why you are justified when you render your verdict,
completely correct when you issue your judgment."

Building Block #2: Accept the pain you have caused and the consequences it brings.

Pornography addiction divides your soul as well as the relationships in your life. Your confession will likely throw your loved ones into a tail-spin.

Be prepared for this.

Seek counsel ahead of time.

Have a friend join you. Take any measures you can take to help your spouse, child, or loved one receive your confession. At the same time, be prepared for immense pain and anger to burst forth from the hurt they will feel.

I cannot overemphasize this point. The revelation or your struggle with pornography is going to hit your loved one like a hammer. They will reel and react in ways that you must absorb.

Their pain does ease – with time, counsel, and the steady re-building of trust - but the consequences may endure for some time. You will need to begin to establish rhythms of trust and surrender that will help rebuild hope and confidence.

Building Block #3: Make a commitment to take concrete action that will move you toward freedom.

Commit to making a host of intentional and steady decisions that remove the vehicles of 'easy input' and establish rhythms of accountability.

I committed to a life of accountability with Melissa and others whom she trusted to help me walk this path.

Here are a few choices I made that helped move me toward freedom:

- Intentional involvement with a counselor or support group that helped me process why I felt the need to escape into the world of porn.
- Consistent rhythms and patterns that rebuilt trust and confidence. For example, my wife had access to my calendar and could call me at any moment and get a report on exactly what I was doing.
- I found a friend that would hold me accountable and encourage me toward freedom.
- I avoided places that might trigger the addiction.
- I installed – and still keep installed – accountability software on every device. My wife keeps the password.

These building blocks require surrender. There is no other way. Life in your own hands has become a mess. You must surrender control and trust others to help you achieve that which you are unable to achieve for yourself.

As you surrender, you then build trust and begin to trust.

As you build trust and begin to trust, you become a person who lives in and longs for the rhythm of surrender.

Before you know it, you are beginning to live with intention, and you are no longer fleeing - as frequently - to the perils of your bloodsucking habit/pattern/addiction.

The cycle is beautiful and life-giving!

Self – Preservation is Not the Place to Stay

From the moment we come out screaming from the womb, to the moment we begin sliding toward the tomb, we are taught the virtue of self-preservation.

While self-preservation is instinctual and, at times, necessary for survival, I am concerned with the underbelly of this instinct.

Decades ago, when I was a child, I did something with a friend that I knew I'd be punished for if my parents ever found out. My friend's father found out and spoke to us about our behavior. When I told him how scared I was of telling my parents, he said, with a smile,

"Son, you need to tell the truth, but you don't always have to tell the whole truth."

Boy did the lesson sink in that day – tell the truth right up to the point where it can get you into trouble. That is what I call self-preservation! Getting right up to the line, but not crossing it and, when you do, intentionally developing a plan to tell a portion of the truth so that you can avoid the fullest responsibility of your actions.

Self-preservation is both a part of nature as well as nurture! As such, self-preservation tends to become the default orientation of many adults – especially those who remain trapped in pornography.

Yes, self-preservation is a natural response that has been habitually nurtured. It is not, however, the place to stay if you hope to rebuild your life from the brokenness porn has caused.

Wondering if You are a Self-preservationist?

If you normally experience one or more of the following reactions to viewing or being caught viewing porn, you might be a self-preservationist:

1. Do you hide all the evidence?
2.
3. Are you deleting your browsing history, covering up your phone history, erasing viewing history, etc.?

4. Do you pretend that someone else did it? When practicing self-preservation it's easy to try and lay the blame somewhere or on someone else. For instance, on a colleague, teenager, spouse, etc.

5. Do you try to minimize what you saw or why you clicked, viewed, or acted out? Any rationalization, at this point, is usually birthed from a desire to protect oneself from the full consequences of one's actions.

6. Do you use the 'Well, at least my acting out wasn't as bad as it was the last time' line when caught? While this acknowledgement is important, it's not the place to start. Starting here reveals a normal desire to avoid the pain of confrontation but fails to allow for the freedom of redemption that accompanies genuine acceptance of the behavior.

If you can say 'yes' to one or more of these, then you may be struggling with the natural tendency toward self-preservation and blame-shifting.

The problem with practicing self-preservation is that it leads into patterns of isolation, deception, and mistrust.

Once trapped in this world, we find it is very, very hard to break free.

In fact, this is what I call the *compounding shame phase* of the addiction. Already shamed by the addiction, we compound our shame by entering a self - preservation pattern.

This pattern is designed to continually hide the addiction.

Shame, invariably, moves one back into the first response of self-preservation and blame-shifting.

From Self-preservation to the Life-giving Rhythms of Honesty, Openness, Perseverance, and Engagement

Honesty. Self-preservation prevents honesty! If you have acted out, or continue to struggle, it's best to be honest with those whom this impacts the most!

Be honest with yourself, the Lord, and your loved ones. This is a difficult place to begin, but if you practice honesty, then you will find that – over time – the deceptive power of porn does decrease.

Openness. Developing a rhythm that is open to scrutiny will help you as you move forward in this walk out of porn. Be sure others have access to your devices. Ask others to hold you accountable, particularly in those areas of known triggers.

Perseverance. Don't give up! I have spoken with countless men who feel like giving in and giving up. Don't swim in that shame. Once you practice honesty and experience openness, then you can assess where you are and reaffirm your desire to be free from porn's pull!

Engagement. Relapse into addiction can lead us into an isolated island of guilt and shame. Don't let that happen. Have an action plan in place that includes re-engaging in meaningful ways with the people you love and those who love you.

Engage in a craft, hobby, the community, your church, a special skill or talent. Engaging into the meaningful people and places God has granted will lead you into a life of honesty, openness, perseverance, and engagement.

These rhythms will birth **HOPE** that porn can never steal and from which you can begin to rebuild your life from the ravages of porn!

Finally, for those who trip-up from time to time. We must answer the question of what to do then!

Does One Bad Moment Make Me A Monster?

I had been porn free for about three months. It was, at that time, the longest I had ever gone without clicking a website, watching a video, or trying to get porn in any form I could.

Then one day I crashed, badly.

All the signs were there, I just didn't see them.

Either that or I simply refused to take note of them.

The triggers were:

1. **Fatigue.**
2. **Isolation.**
3. **Boredom.**

In a moment of weakness, I 'clicked' a site and woke, about an hour later from a porn induced stupor, wondering where I had been, what I had done and, most importantly, why I had done what I'd done.

I was angry.

I was embarrassed.

I was sad.

I was miserable.

All the purity I had enjoyed? Gone. In one bad moment, with one click of a mouse and one surf on the web, months of purity were flushed down the drain.

If you've ever battled pornography addiction, then you can probably relate to my experience. You've made it a day, a week, a month or more without feeding the addiction. Then, one day, you stumble.

You fall.

You crash.

The question I want to ask, and I think it's an important one for us, is this:

Does one bad moment make me a monster?

We feel like it, don't we?

We feel the shame and guilt.

We isolate ourselves, dampen our emotional antenna and slink emotionlessly along.

Zombie-like we wander, tethered to the haunting fear that we will be exposed and bound by the relenting anxiety that we cannot stop, wondering when the monster will rear its menacing head and come growling back for more.

We begin to live from a place of fear and anxiety. This place from which we live colors every relationship and experience with terrifying and crippling outcomes.

We lash out at the people we love.

We push away those who try to get into our heart.

We pretend we are well while we sour inside.

But what if *one bad moment* doesn't make you/me a monster? What if that's a lie the addiction has contrived to keep us trapped and hold us back?

What if *one bad moment* really could be just **one** bad moment and not a season of doubt, distortion and despair?

What if *one bad moment* doesn't have to lead to fear and anxiety?

What if *one bad moment* could actually become a moment you build from rather than one in which you stay trapped?

What if you were able to implement one or two small steps - in that one moment – that would give you some traction on an otherwise rocky terrain?

Take hope. I believe your one bad moment can be the moment you turn your addiction around!

You don't have to take major leaps, either. Just simple, but consistent, steps.

I am, as one who has experienced *one bad moment*, going to offer a few steps that have been meaningful to me.

1. **Stop and tell someone on whom you can depend.** This is crucial. That's why I make reference to it in nearly every article I write. You have to let someone you trust know that you have slipped and fallen again. I don't care if your latest 'episode' was one small click or a tortuous journey into the darkest side of your soul.

Seriously! No matter how badly you have stumbled, there is someone in your life who can listen to you and bring hope to your soul. Tell them. If you don't have that person, let us know. We will try to provide resources to help you make this possible.

2. **Get up and do something.** Get around people as quickly as you can. Over-schedule your time for the next day or two. Be careful where you go because porn triggers lurk around every corner.

Just do your best *not to* find yourself alone for any extended amount of time as you begin your journey back to freedom! Isolation is a seedbed for addiction.

3. **Block those mechanisms that exploit your addiction.** When I am struggling, I disable the apps (primarily the social media apps) on my phone. I also restrict my computer usage to public places.

If your trigger is a certain section of town, an old phone number, a massage parlor, a 'fitness' or 'bikini' page you enjoy visiting on the web, then stay away from it (them).

You know your triggers; put in safe guards and reroute your life for a while!

4. **Find a recovery resource (workbook, textbook, small group, web conference) and begin to work your way through it.** You need to begin to replace the addiction with some healthy and life giving messages of hope and renewal.

I would recommend a daily program of recovery and restoration. Recovery programs have been a crucial part of my own journey into freedom and my life apart from porn!

Okay, that's it.

Pick one.

You can take this step.

Your most recent *one bad moment* may or may not be your last *one bad moment*.

10 THE HOPE-FILLED FORTY-DAY FREEDOM JOURNEY

AN INVITATION TO AN ONGOING AND EVER-CHANGING JOURNEY OF DENIAL AND DELIGHT.

Forty-Day Freedom Journey Overview

This forty-day Freedom Journey of delighting in our eternal attractions and denial of our modern attachments includes a daily rhythm that, when practiced, can help one break free from porn's power!

Each day falls into three specific rhythms:

1. Beginning the day by delighting in our eternal attractions. We start by focusing on hope and a biblical vision for the 'good life' which God desires we enjoy. Some days will combine activities, hobbies, and projects that are specific to our own talents and gifts.

2. Committing to denying ourselves some aspects of modern life. This commitment is designed to raise awareness regarding our habits and assist us in freeing ourselves of addictions. Most of the commitments are related to our use of technology. We focus on technology because the porn

industry is very clear that the medium they most prefer is technology. If porn is the vehicle that drives in and wrecks life, then technology is the highway on which it drives!

3. Ending the day by delighting in our eternal attractions. This practice will often be a repeat of the morning exercise and enables us to ease into our night enjoying freedom as we focus on God's joy in us and His delight over us!

This Freedom Journey doesn't require perfection, merely a willingness to practice! If you miss a day, no sweat. Just pick up on the next day. As you move through the daily challenges you'll find that they are incremental and require more commitment over time.

As such, missing a day or two shouldn't discourage you. Stay with it no matter what. The whole challenge is designed to be completed, but if it takes fifty or sixty days, that's fine! Just don't give up!

Do you want to be free?

Do you want to discover and enjoy a hope-filled journey into the fullness Christ offers?

Then take the challenge today.

Forty-Day Freedom Journey

DAY ONE

Begin the Day by Delighting in an Eternal Attraction

Take 3 – 5 minutes to meditate on, pray over, and internalize Jesus' words in Matthew Chapter 22:

> *34 But when the Pharisees heard that he had silenced the Sadducees with his reply, they met together to question him again. 35 One of them, an expert in religious law, tried to trap him with this question: 36 "Teacher, which is the most important commandment in the law of Moses?" 37 Jesus replied, "'You must love the Lord your God with all your heart, all your soul, and all your mind.' 38 This is the first and greatest commandment. 39 A second is equally important: 'Love your neighbor as yourself.' 40 The entire law and all the demands of the prophets are based on these two commandments."*

During the Day - Denial of a Modern Attachment

DAY 1: SCREENS DOWN

For today's challenge we are going to turn ALL screens off fifteen minutes before bedtime. This means smart phones, televisions, computers, etc. Spend this time focusing on today's delight and just reflecting on the day and preparing for tomorrow. You can do this!

End the Day by Delighting in an Eternal Attraction

Take 3 – 5 minutes to meditate on, pray over, and internalize Jesus' words in Matthew Chapter 22:

> *34 But when the Pharisees heard that he had silenced the Sadducees with his reply, they met together to question him again. 35 One of them, an expert in religious law, tried to trap him with this question: 36 "Teacher, which is the most important commandment in the law of Moses?"37 Jesus replied, "'You must love the Lord your God with all your heart, all your soul, and all your mind.' 38 This is the first and greatest commandment. 39 A second is equally important: 'Love your neighbor as yourself.' 40 The entire law and all the law."*

DAY TWO

Begin the Day by Delighting in an Eternal Attraction
Take 3 – 5 minutes to meditate on, pray over, and internalize Jesus' words in Matthew Chapter 22:

34 But when the Pharisees heard that he had silenced the Sadducees with his reply, they met together to question him again. 35 One of them, an expert in religious law, tried to trap him with this question: 36 "Teacher, which is the most important commandment in the law of Moses?"

37 Jesus replied, "'You must love the Lord your God with all your heart, all your soul, and all your mind.' 38 This is the first and greatest commandment. 39 A second is equally important: 'Love your neighbor as yourself.' 40 The entire law and all the demands of the prophets are based on these two commandments."

During the Day - Denial of a Modern Attachment
DAY 2: SOCIAL MEDIA DETOX

For today's challenge we are going to disable our notifications and go three hours without viewing, responding to, or checking in with our social media apps. All of the apps you lean on should be included in this 3-hour challenge window.

End the Day by Delighting in an Eternal Attraction
Take 3 – 5 minutes to meditate on, pray over, and internalize Jesus' words in Matthew Chapter 22:

34 But when the Pharisees heard that he had silenced the Sadducees with his reply, they met together to question him again. 35 One of them, an expert in religious law, tried to trap him with this question: 36 "Teacher, which is the most important commandment in the law of Moses?"

37 Jesus replied, "'You must love the Lord your God with all your heart, all your soul, and all your mind.' 38 This is the first and greatest commandment. 39 A second is equally important: 'Love your neighbor as yourself.' 40 The entire law and all the demands of the prophets are based on these two commandments."

DAY THREE

Begin the Day by Delighting in Eternal Attraction
Take 3 – 5 minutes to meditate on, pray over, and internalize Jesus' words in Matthew Chapter 22:

34 But when the Pharisees heard that he had silenced the Sadducees with his reply, they met together to question him again. 35 One of them, an expert in religious law, tried to trap him with this question: 36 "Teacher, which is the most important commandment in the law of Moses?"

37 Jesus replied, "'You must love the Lord your God with all your heart, all your soul, and all your mind.' 38 This is the first and greatest commandment. 39 A second is equally important: 'Love your neighbor as yourself.' 40 The entire law and all the demands of the prophets are based on these two commandments."

During the Day - Denial of a Modern Attachment
DAY 3: OPEN AREAS ONLY

Today's challenge is to keep our screens out in the open at all times. In other words, no screens behind closed doors! This includes bedrooms, bathrooms, office spaces, etc. You will be amazed by how difficult this one will be to remember!

End the Day by Delighting in an Eternal Attraction
Take 3 – 5 minutes to meditate on, pray over, and internalize Jesus' words in Matthew Chapter 22:

34 But when the Pharisees heard that he had silenced the Sadducees with his reply, they met together to question him again. 35 One of them, an expert in religious law, tried to trap him with this question: 36 "Teacher, which is the most important commandment in the law of Moses?" 37 Jesus replied, "'You must love the Lord your God with all your heart, all your soul, and all your mind.' 38 This is the first and greatest commandment. 39 A second is equally important: 'Love your neighbor as yourself.' 40 The entire law and all the demands of the prophets are based on these two commandments."

DAY FOUR

Begin the Day by Delighting in Eternal Attraction
Take 3 – 5 minutes to meditate on, pray over, and internalize Jesus' words in Matthew Chapter 22:

34 But when the Pharisees heard that he had silenced the Sadducees with his reply, they met together to question him again. 35 One of them, an expert in religious law, tried to trap him with this question: 36 "Teacher, which is the most important commandment in the law of Moses?" 37 Jesus replied, "'You must love the Lord your God with all your heart, all your soul, and all your mind.' 38 This is the first and greatest commandment. 39 A second is equally important: 'Love your neighbor as yourself.' 40 The entire law and all the demands of the prophets are based on these two commandments."

During the Day - Denial of a Modern Attachment
DAY 4: GAMING-FREE ZONE
We spend too much time online these days. Some stats indicate that teens spend about nine hours a day on social media apps. The bulk of that time is spent on gaming. Today's challenge is to spend two-plus hours you'd normally be spending gaming on some other activity. You may even try something outdoors!

End the Day by Delighting in an Eternal Attraction
Take 3 – 5 minutes to meditate on, pray over, and internalize Jesus' words in Matthew Chapter 22:

34 But when the Pharisees heard that he had silenced the Sadducees with his reply, they met together to question him again. 35 One of them, an expert in religious law, tried to trap him with this question: 36 "Teacher, which is the most important commandment in the law of Moses?" 37 Jesus replied, "'You must love the Lord your God with all your heart, all your soul, and all your mind.' 38 This is the first and greatest commandment. 39 A second is equally important: 'Love your neighbor as yourself.' 40 The entire law and all the demands of the prophets are based on these two commandments."

DAY FIVE

Begin the Day by Delighting in Eternal Attraction
Take 3 – 5 minutes to meditate on, pray over, and internalize Jesus' words in Matthew Chapter 22:

34 But when the Pharisees heard that he had silenced the Sadducees with his reply, they met together to question him again. 35 One of them, an expert in religious law, tried to trap him with this question: 36 "Teacher, which is the most important commandment in the law of Moses?" 37 Jesus replied, "'You must love the Lord your God with all your heart, all your soul, and all your mind.' 38 This is the first and greatest commandment. 39 A second is equally important: 'Love your neighbor as yourself.' 40 The entire law and all the demands of the prophets are based on these two commandments."

During the Day - Denial of a Modern Attachment
DAY 5: BREAKAWAY DAY

Today's challenge is to make a clean break from all social media! We will start small and try to stay off of screens and social media for a one – two hour period of time.

End the Day by Delighting in an Eternal Attraction
Take 3 – 5 minutes to meditate on, pray over, and internalize Jesus' words in Matthew Chapter 22:

34 But when the Pharisees heard that he had silenced the Sadducees with his reply, they met together to question him again. 35 One of them, an expert in religious law, tried to trap him with this question: 36 "Teacher, which is the most important commandment in the law of Moses?" 37 Jesus replied, "'You must love the Lord your God with all your heart, all your soul, and all your mind.' 38 This is the first and greatest commandment. 39 A second is equally important: 'Love your neighbor as yourself.' 40 The entire law and all the demands of the prophets are based on these two commandments."

DAY SIX

Begin the Day by Delighting in Eternal Attraction
Take 3 – 5 minutes Create a short list of three activities and/or hobbies you'd like to do or try for the first time. Make every effort to spend an hour a day experiencing or focusing on one of the activities on your list.

During the Day - Denial of a Modern Attachment
DAY 6: SURF AND SHOP-FREE ZONES

Today's challenge is to dedicate a portion of your day, begin with a two – three hour increment, and determine not to surf or shop on the web during that time!

End the Day by Delighting in an Eternal Attraction
Take 3 – 5 minutes to meditate on, pray over, and internalize Jesus' words in Matthew Chapter 6:

"Don't store up treasures here on earth, where moths eat them and rust destroys them, and where thieves break in and steal. [20] Store your treasures in heaven, where moths and rust cannot destroy, and thieves do not break in and steal. [21] Wherever your treasure is, there the desires of your heart will also be." [22] "Your eye is like a lamp that provides light for your body. When your eye is healthy, your whole body is filled with light.

DAY SEVEN

Begin the Day by Delighting in an Eternal Attraction
Take 3 – 5 minutes create a short list of three activities and/or hobbies you'd like to do or try for the first time. Make every effort to spend an hour a day experiencing or focusing on one of the activities on your list.

During the Day – Denial of a Modern Attachment
DAY 7: SOCIAL MEDIA DETOX DAY

For today's challenge we are going to disable our notifications and go three hours without viewing, responding to, or checking in with our social media apps. All of the apps you lean on should be included in this 3-hour challenge window.

End the Day by Delighting in an Eternal Attraction
Take 3 – 5 minutes to meditate on, pray over, and Internalize Jesus' words in Matthew Chapter 6:

"Don't store up treasures here on earth, where moths eat them and rust destroys them, and where thieves break in and steal. [20] Store your treasures in heaven, where moths and rust cannot destroy, and thieves do not break in and steal. [21] Wherever your treasure is, there the desires of your heart will also be.

[22] "Your eye is like a lamp that provides light for your body. When your eye is healthy, your whole body is filled with light."

DAY EIGHT

Begin the Day by Delighting in an Eternal Attraction
Take 3 – 5 minutes create a short list of three activities and/or hobbies you'd like to do or try for the first time. Make every effort to spend an hour a day experiencing or focusing on one of the activities on your list.

During the Day – Denial of a Modern Attachment
DAY 8: TALK-ONLY TEXT-FREE ZONE

Today's challenge is to 'text' less and 'talk' more. Here's how it works. When you get a message today, spend time calling and talking or just wait until tomorrow to respond. You may want to begin by committing two – three hours to this and allow the other hours to remain as they are.

End the Day by Delighting in an Eternal Attraction
Take 3 – 5 minutes to meditate on, pray over, and Internalize Jesus' words in Matthew Chapter 6:

"Don't store up treasures here on earth, where moths eat them and rust destroys them, and where thieves break in and steal. [20] Store your treasures in heaven, where moths and rust cannot destroy, and thieves do not break in and steal. [21] Wherever your treasure is, there the desires of your heart will also be.

[22] "Your eye is like a lamp that provides light for your body. When your eye is healthy, your whole body is filled with light."

DAY NINE

Begin the Day by Delighting in an Eternal Attraction
Take 3 – 5 minutes create a short list of three activities and/or hobbies you'd like to do or try for the first time. Make every effort to spend an hour a day experiencing or focusing on one of the activities on your list.

During the Day – Denial of a Modern Attachment
DAY 9: TELEVISION-FREE ZONE

Today's challenge is to commit a portion of your day to being a 'TV-free zone.' Let's start slow by committing one – two hours of today! You may want to focus on one of your hobbies during this time!

End the Day by Delighting in an Eternal Attraction
Take 3 – 5 minutes to meditate on, pray over, and Internalize Jesus' words in Matthew Chapter 6:

"Don't store up treasures here on earth, where moths eat them and rust destroys them, and where thieves break in and steal. [20] Store your treasures in heaven, where moths and rust cannot destroy, and thieves do not break in and steal. [21] Wherever your treasure is, there the desires of your heart will also be.

[22] "Your eye is like a lamp that provides light for your body. When your eye is healthy, your whole body is filled with light."

DAY TEN

Begin the Day by Delighting in an Eternal Attraction
Take 3 – 5 minutes create a short list of three activities and/or hobbies you'd like to do or try for the first time. Make every effort to spend an hour a day experiencing or focusing on one of the activities on your list.

During the Day – Denial of a Modern Attachment
DAY 10: BREAKAWAY DAY

Today's challenge is to make a clean break from all social media! We will start small and try to stay off of screens and social media for a one – two hour period of time.

End the Day by Delighting in an Eternal Attraction
Take 3 – 5 minutes to meditate on, pray over, and Internalize Jesus' words in Matthew Chapter 6:

"Don't store up treasures here on earth, where moths eat them and rust destroys them, and where thieves break in and steal. [20] Store your treasures in heaven, where moths and rust cannot destroy, and thieves do not break in and steal. [21] Wherever your treasure is, there the desires of your heart will also be.

[22] "Your eye is like a lamp that provides light for your body. When your eye is healthy, your whole body is filled with light."

DAY ELEVEN

Begin the Day by Delighting in an Eternal Attraction
Meditate on and internalize the Apostle Paul's words in Romans 12:

And so, dear brothers and sisters, I plead with you to give your bodies to God because of all he has done for you. Let them be a living and holy sacrifice—the kind he will find acceptable. This is truly the way to worship him. 2 Don't copy the behavior and customs of this world, but let God transform you into a new person by changing the way you think. Then you will learn to know God's will for you, which is good and pleasing and perfect.

During the Day – Denial of a Modern Attachment
DAY 11: SCREENS DOWN

For today's challenge we are going to begin our day and then end our day with screens off for thirty minutes. This means smart phones, televisions, computers, etc. Spend this time – at the beginning and end of the day – focusing on today's delight and just reflecting on and preparing for the day ahead.

End the Day by Delighting in an Eternal Attraction
Meditate on and internalize the Apostle Paul's words in Romans 12:

And so, dear brothers and sisters, I plead with you to give your bodies to God because of all he has done for you. Let them be a living and holy sacrifice—the kind he will find acceptable. This is truly the way to worship him. 2 Don't copy the behavior and customs of this world, but let God transform you into a new person by changing the way you think. Then you will learn to know God's will for you, which is good and pleasing and perfect.

DAY TWELVE

Begin the Day by Delighting in an Eternal Attraction
Meditate on and internalize the Apostle Paul's words in Romans 12:

And so, dear brothers and sisters, I plead with you to give your bodies to God because of all he has done for you. Let them be a living and holy sacrifice—the kind he will find acceptable. This is truly the way to worship him. 2 Don't copy the behavior and customs of this world, but let God transform you into a new person by changing the way you think. Then you will learn to know God's will for you, which is good and pleasing and perfect.

During the Day – Denial of a Modern Attachment
DAY: SOCIAL MEDIA DETOX DAY

For today's challenge we are going to disable our notification and go four hours without viewing, responding to, or checking in with our social media apps. All of the apps you lean on should be included in this four-hour challenge window.

End the Day by Delighting in an Eternal Attraction
Meditate on and internalize the Apostle Paul's words in Romans 12:

And so, dear brothers and sisters, I plead with you to give your bodies to God because of all he has done for you. Let them be a living and holy sacrifice—the kind he will find acceptable. This is truly the way to worship him. 2 Don't copy the behavior and customs of this world, but let God transform you into a new person by changing the way you think. Then you will learn to know God's will for you, which is good and pleasing and perfect.

DAY THIRTEEN

Begin the Day by Delighting in an Eternal Attraction
Meditate on and internalize the Apostle Paul's words in Romans 12:

And so, dear brothers and sisters, I plead with you to give your bodies to God because of all he has done for you. Let them be a living and holy sacrifice—the kind he will find acceptable. This is truly the way to worship him. 2 Don't copy the behavior and customs of this world, but let God transform you into a new person by changing the way you think. Then you will learn to know God's will for you, which is good and pleasing and perfect.

During the Day – Denial of a Modern Attachment
DAY 13: OPEN AREAS ONLY

Today's challenge is to keep our screens out in the open at all times. In other words, no screens behind closed doors! This includes bedrooms, bathrooms, office spaces, etc. You will be amazed by how difficult this one will be to remember!

End the Day by Delighting in an Eternal Attraction
Meditate on and internalize the Apostle Paul's words in Romans 12:

And so, dear brothers and sisters, I plead with you to give your bodies to God because of all he has done for you. Let them be a living and holy sacrifice—the kind he will find acceptable. This is truly the way to worship him. 2 Don't copy the behavior and customs of this world, but let God transform you into a new person by changing the way you think. Then you will learn to know God's will for you, which is good and pleasing and perfect.

DAY FOURTEEN

Begin the Day by Delighting in an Eternal Attraction
Meditate on and internalize the Apostle Paul's words in Romans 12:

And so, dear brothers and sisters, I plead with you to give your bodies to God because of all he has done for you. Let them be a living and holy sacrifice—the kind he will find acceptable. This is truly the way to worship him. 2 Don't copy the behavior and customs of this world, but let God transform you into a new person by changing the way you think. Then you will learn to know God's will for you, which is good and pleasing and perfect.

During the Day – Denial of a Modern Attachment
DAY 14: GAMING-FREE ZONES

We spend too much time online these days. Some stats indicate that we (teens especially) spend about nine hours a day on social media apps. The bulk of that time is spent on gaming. Today's challenge is to spend four hours you'd normally be spending gaming on some other activity. You may even try something outdoors!

End the Day by Delighting in an Eternal Attraction
Meditate on and internalize the Apostle Paul's words in Romans 12:

And so, dear brothers and sisters, I plead with you to give your bodies to God because of all he has done for you. Let them be a living and holy sacrifice—the kind he will find acceptable. This is truly the way to worship him. 2 Don't copy the behavior and customs of this world, but let God transform you into a new person by changing the way you think. Then you will learn to know God's will for you, which is good and pleasing and perfect.

DAY FIFTEEN

Begin the Day by Delighting in an Eternal Attraction
Meditate on and internalize the Apostle Paul's words in Romans 12:

And so, dear brothers and sisters, I plead with you to give your bodies to God because of all he has done for you. Let them be a living and holy sacrifice—the kind he will find acceptable. This is truly the way to worship him. 2 Don't copy the behavior and customs of this world, but let God transform you into a new person by changing the way you think. Then you will learn to know God's will for you, which is good and pleasing and perfect.

During the Day – Denial of a Modern Attachment
DAY 15: BREAKAWAY DAY

Today's challenge is to make a clean break from all social media! We will start small and try to stay off of screens and social media for a three - four hour period of time.

End the Day by Delighting in an Eternal Attraction
Meditate on and internalize the Apostle Paul's words in Romans 12:

And so, dear brothers and sisters, I plead with you to give your bodies to God because of all he has done for you. Let them be a living and holy sacrifice—the kind he will find acceptable. This is truly the way to worship him. 2 Don't copy the behavior and customs of this world, but let God transform you into a new person by changing the way you think. Then you will learn to know God's will for you, which is good and pleasing and perfect.

DAY SIXTEEN

Begin the Day by Delighting in an Eternal Attraction

Spend time developing or experiencing the activities and/or hobbies you crafted during days five through ten of this challenge. Make every effort to spend an hour a day experiencing or focusing on one of the activities on your list.

During the Day – Denial of a Modern Attachment
DAY 16: SURF AND SHOP-FREE ZONES

Today's challenge is to dedicate a portion of your day, begin with a three - four hour increment, and determine not to surf or shop on the web during that time!

End the Day by Delighting in an Eternal Attraction
Meditate on and internalize the Apostle Paul's words in Romans 12:

And so, dear brothers and sisters, I plead with you to give your bodies to God because of all he has done for you. Let them be a living and holy sacrifice—the kind he will find acceptable. This is truly the way to worship him. 2 Don't copy the behavior and customs of this world, but let God transform you into a new person by changing the way you think. Then you will learn to know God's will for you, which is good and pleasing and perfect.

DAY SEVENTEEN

Begin the Day by Delighting in an Eternal Attraction
Spend time developing or experiencing the activities and/or hobbies you crafted during days five through ten of this challenge. Make every effort to spend an hour a day experiencing or focusing on one of the activities on your list.

During the Day – Denial of a Modern Attachment
DAY 17: SOCIAL MEDIA DETOX DAY

For today's challenge we are going to disable our notifications and go four hours without viewing, responding to, or checking in with our social media apps. All of the apps you lean on should be included in this four-hour challenge window.

End the Day by Delighting in an Eternal Attraction
Meditate on and internalize the Apostle Paul's words in Romans 12:

And so, dear brothers and sisters, I plead with you to give your bodies to God because of all he has done for you. Let them be a living and holy sacrifice—the kind he will find acceptable. This is truly the way to worship him. 2 Don't copy the behavior and customs of this world, but let God transform you into a new person by changing the way you think. Then you will learn to know God's will for you, which is good and pleasing and perfect.

DAY EIGHTEEN

Begin the Day by Delighting in an Eternal Attraction
Spend time developing or experiencing the activities and/or hobbies you crafted during days five through ten of this challenge. Make every effort to spend an hour a day experiencing or focusing on one of the activities on your list.

During the Day – Denial of a Modern Attachment
DAY 18: TALK-ONLY TEXT-FREE ZONES

Today's challenge is to 'text' less and 'talk' more. Here's how it works. When you get a message today, spend time calling and talking or just wait until tomorrow to respond. You may want to begin by committing four hours to this and allow the other hours to remain as they are.

End the Day by Delighting in an Eternal Attraction
Meditate on and internalize the Apostle Paul's words in Romans 12:

And so, dear brothers and sisters, I plead with you to give your bodies to God because of all he has done for you. Let them be a living and holy sacrifice—the kind he will find acceptable. This is truly the way to worship him. 2 Don't copy the behavior and customs of this world, but let God transform you into a new person by changing the way you think. Then you will learn to know God's will for you, which is good and pleasing and perfect.

DAY NINETEEN

Begin the Day by Delighting in an Eternal Attraction
Spend time developing or experiencing the activities and/or hobbies you crafted during days five through ten of this challenge. Make every effort to spend an hour a day experiencing or focusing on one of the activities on your list.

During the Day – Denial of a Modern Attachment
DAY 19: TV-FREE ZONES
Today's challenge is to commit a portion of your day to being a 'TV free zone.' Let's start slow by committing four hours of today! You may want to focus on one of your hobbies during this time!

End the Day by Delighting in an Eternal Attraction
Meditate on and internalize the Apostle Paul's words in Romans 12:

And so, dear brothers and sisters, I plead with you to give your bodies to God because of all he has done for you. Let them be a living and holy sacrifice—the kind he will find acceptable. This is truly the way to worship him. 2 Don't copy the behavior and customs of this world, but let God transform you into a new person by changing the way you think. Then you will learn to know God's will for you, which is good and pleasing and perfect.

DAY TWENTY

Begin the Day by Delighting in an Eternal Attraction
Spend time developing or experiencing the activities and/or hobbies you crafted during days five through ten of this challenge. Make every effort to spend an hour a day experiencing or focusing on one of the activities on your list.

During the Day – Denial of a Modern Attachment
DAY 20: BREAKAWAY DAY

Today's challenge is to make a clean break from all social media! We will start small and try to stay off of screens and social media for a four-hour period of time.

End the Day by Delighting in an Eternal Attraction
Meditate on and internalize the Apostle Paul's words in Romans 12:

And so, dear brothers and sisters, I plead with you to give your bodies to God because of all he has done for you. Let them be a living and holy sacrifice—the kind he will find acceptable. This is truly the way to worship him. 2 Don't copy the behavior and customs of this world, but let God transform you into a new person by changing the way you think. Then you will learn to know God's will for you, which is good and pleasing and perfect.

DAY TWENTY ONE

Begin the Day by Delighting in an Eternal Attraction
Meditate on and internalize the Apostle Paul's words in I Corinthians 10:

¹² If you think you are standing strong, be careful not to fall. ¹³ The temptations in your life are no different from what others experience. And God is faithful. He will not allow the temptation to be more than you can stand. When you are tempted, he will show you a way out so that you can endure. ¹⁴ So, my dear friends, flee from the worship of idols.

During the Day – Denial of a Modern Attachment
DAY 21: SCREENS DOWN

For today's challenge we are going to begin our day and then end our day with screens off for sixty minutes. This means smart phones, televisions, computers, etc. Spend this time – at the beginning and end of the day – focusing on today's delight and just reflecting on and preparing for the day ahead.

End the Day by Delighting in an Eternal Attraction
Meditate on and internalize the Apostle Paul's words in I Corinthians 10:

¹² If you think you are standing strong, be careful not to fall. ¹³ The temptations in your life are no different from what others experience. And God is faithful. He will not allow the temptation to be more than you can stand. When you are tempted, he will show you a way out so that you can endure. ¹⁴ So, my dear friends, flee from the worship of idols.

DAY TWENTY TWO

Begin the Day by Delighting in an Eternal Attraction
Meditate on and internalize the Apostle Paul's words in I Corinthians 10:

[12] If you think you are standing strong, be careful not to fall. [13] The temptations in your life are no different from what others experience. And God is faithful. He will not allow the temptation to be more than you can stand. When you are tempted, he will show you a way out so that you can endure. [14] So, my dear friends, flee from the worship of idols.

During the Day – Denial of a Modern Attachment
DAY 22: SOCIAL MEDIA DETOX DAY

For today's challenge we are going to disable our notifications and go four hours without viewing, responding to, or checking in with our social media apps. All of the apps you lean on should be included in this six-hour challenge window.

End the Day by Delighting in an Eternal Attraction
Meditate on and internalize the Apostle Paul's words in I Corinthians 10:

[12] If you think you are standing strong, be careful not to fall. [13] The temptations in your life are no different from what others experience. And God is faithful. He will not allow the temptation to be more than you can stand. When you are tempted, he will show you a way out so that you can endure. [14] So, my dear friends, flee from the worship of idols.

DAY TWENTY THREE

Begin the Day by Delighting in an Eternal Attraction
Meditate on and internalize the Apostle Paul's words in I Corinthians 10:

^{12} If you think you are standing strong, be careful not to fall. ^{13} The temptations in your life are no different from what others experience. And God is faithful. He will not allow the temptation to be more than you can stand. When you are tempted, he will show you a way out so that you can endure. ^{14} So, my dear friends, flee from the worship of idols.

During the Day – Denial of a Modern Attachment
DAY 23: OPEN AREAS ONLY

Today's challenge is to keep our screens out in the open at all times. In other words, no screens behind closed doors! This includes bedrooms, bathrooms, office spaces, etc. You will be amazed by how difficult this one will be to remember!

End the Day by Delighting in an Eternal Attraction
Meditate on and internalize the Apostle Paul's words in I Corinthians 10:

^{12} If you think you are standing strong, be careful not to fall. ^{13} The temptations in your life are no different from what others experience. And God is faithful. He will not allow the temptation to be more than you can stand. When you are tempted, he will show you a way out so that you can endure. ^{14} So, my dear friends, flee from the worship of idols.

DAY TWENTY FOUR

Begin the Day by Delighting in an Eternal Attraction
Meditate on and internalize the Apostle Paul's words in I Corinthians 10:

[12] If you think you are standing strong, be careful not to fall. [13] The temptations in your life are no different from what others experience. And God is faithful. He will not allow the temptation to be more than you can stand. When you are tempted, he will show you a way out so that you can endure. [14] So, my dear friends, flee from the worship of idols.

During the Day – Denial of a Modern Attachment
DAY 24: GAMING-FREE ZONES

We spend too much time online these days. Some stats indicate that teens spend about nine hours a day on social media apps. The bulk of that time is spent on gaming. Today's challenge is to spend nine hours you'd normally be spending gaming on some other activity. You may even try something outdoors!

End the Day by Delighting in an Eternal Attraction
Meditate on and internalize the Apostle Paul's words in I Corinthians 10:

[12] If you think you are standing strong, be careful not to fall. [13] The temptations in your life are no different from what others experience. And God is faithful. He will not allow the temptation to be more than you can stand. When you are tempted, he will show you a way out so that you can endure. [14] So, my dear friends, flee from the worship of idols.

DAY TWENTY FIVE

Begin the Day by Delighting in an Eternal Attraction
Meditate on and internalize the Apostle Paul's words in I Corinthians 10:

¹² If you think you are standing strong, be careful not to fall. ¹³ The temptations in your life are no different from what others experience. And God is faithful. He will not allow the temptation to be more than you can stand. When you are tempted, he will show you a way out so that you can endure. ¹⁴ So, my dear friends, flee from the worship of idols.

During the Day – Denial of a Modern Attachment
DAY 25: BREAKAWAY DAY

Today's challenge is to make a clean break from all social media! We will start small and try to stay off of screens and social media for a six - nine hour period of time.

End the Day by Delighting in an Eternal Attraction
Meditate on and internalize the Apostle Paul's words in I Corinthians 10:

¹² If you think you are standing strong, be careful not to fall. ¹³ The temptations in your life are no different from what others experience. And God is faithful. He will not allow the temptation to be more than you can stand. When you are tempted, he will show you a way out so that you can endure. ¹⁴ So, my dear friends, flee from the worship of idols.

DAY TWENTY SIX

Begin the Day by Delighting in an Eternal Attraction
Meditate on and internalize the Apostle Paul's words in I Corinthians 10:

¹² If you think you are standing strong, be careful not to fall. ¹³ The temptations in your life are no different from what others experience. And God is faithful. He will not allow the temptation to be more than you can stand. When you are tempted, he will show you a way out so that you can endure. ¹⁴ So, my dear friends, flee from the worship of idols.

During the Day – Denial of a Modern Attachment
DAY 26: ONE SCREEN AT A TIME

Today's challenge will raise awareness regarding how often we have more than one screen open or active at a time. The multiple-screen realty, we've grown accustomed to has created less focused and more highly distracted individuals and culture. Such cultural and personal realities contribute toward us being victimized by the easy diversion porn offers. So, today it's 'one screen at a time' day. This means that when your computer is on, your phone needs to be off. Or, if you are watching a movie, your computer should be turned off and your phone should be inaccessible. Well, you get the idea! Go for it!

End the Day by Delighting in an Eternal Attraction
Meditate on and internalize the Apostle Paul's words in I Corinthians 10:

¹² If you think you are standing strong, be careful not to fall. ¹³ The temptations in your life are no different from what others experience. And God is faithful. He will not allow the temptation to be more than you can stand. When you are tempted, he will show you a way out so that you can endure. ¹⁴ So, my dear friends, flee from the worship of idols.

DAY TWENTY SEVEN

Begin the Day by Delighting in an Eternal Attraction
Meditate on and internalize the Apostle Paul's words in I Corinthians 10:

^{12} If you think you are standing strong, be careful not to fall. ^{13} The temptations in your life are no different from what others experience. And God is faithful. He will not allow the temptation to be more than you can stand. When you are tempted, he will show you a way out so that you can endure. ^{14} So, my dear friends, flee from the worship of idols.

During the Day – Denial of a Modern Attachment
DAY 27: POSITIVE INPUT ONLY

Today's challenge invites us to 'turn off' any input that is negative and demeaning. Many of us listen to song lyrics that demean others. We often involve ourselves in conversations that tear others down. We love the social media sites that are hyper-critical and mean-spirited. We listen to music, watch movies and television programs, etc., that accentuate and exploit the worst parts of humanity. For one day we are going to say 'no' to all such input.

End the Day by Delighting in an Eternal Attraction
Meditate on and internalize the Apostle Paul's words in I Corinthians 10:

^{12} If you think you are standing strong, be careful not to fall. ^{13} The temptations in your life are no different from what others experience. And God is faithful. He will not allow the temptation to be more than you can stand. When you are tempted, he will show you a way out so that you can endure. ^{14} So, my dear friends, flee from the worship of idols.

DAY TWENTY EIGHT

Begin the Day by Delighting in an Eternal Attraction
Meditate on and internalize the Apostle Paul's words in I Corinthians 10:

[12] If you think you are standing strong, be careful not to fall. [13] The temptations in your life are no different from what others experience. And God is faithful. He will not allow the temptation to be more than you can stand. When you are tempted, he will show you a way out so that you can endure. [14] So, my dear friends, flee from the worship of idols.

During the Day – Denial of a Modern Attachment
DAY 28: SOCIAL MEDIA DETOX

For today's challenge we are going to disable our notifications and go six hours without viewing, responding to, or checking in with our social media apps. All of the apps you lean on should be included in this six-hour-challenge window.

End the Day by Delighting in an Eternal Attraction
Meditate on and internalize the Apostle Paul's words in I Corinthians 10:

[12] If you think you are standing strong, be careful not to fall. [13] The temptations in your life are no different from what others experience. And God is faithful. He will not allow the temptation to be more than you can stand. When you are tempted, he will show you a way out so that you can endure. [14] So, my dear friends, flee from the worship of idols.

DAY TWENTY NINE

Begin the Day by Delighting in an Eternal Attraction
Meditate on and internalize the Apostle Paul's words in I Corinthians 10:

¹² If you think you are standing strong, be careful not to fall. ¹³ The temptations in your life are no different from what others experience. And God is faithful. He will not allow the temptation to be more than you can stand. When you are tempted, he will show you a way out so that you can endure. ¹⁴ So, my dear friends, flee from the worship of idols.

During the Day – Denial of a Modern Attachment
DAY 29: PRACTICING GRATITUDE THROUGHOUT THE DAY

Today's challenge invites us to go through our day with a particular focus on being grateful for what we have and where we are in life. Shifting our focus toward gratitude might give us greater clarity on our addictions and struggles. Specifically, take a few minutes and jot down three – five reasons you have to be thankful. Carry those reasons with you throughout your day. Porn leverages ingratitude and tricks us to click on what it offers to ease the pain.

End the Day by Delighting in an Eternal Attraction
Meditate on and internalize the Apostle Paul's words in I Corinthians 10:

¹² If you think you are standing strong, be careful not to fall. ¹³ The temptations in your life are no different from what others experience. And God is faithful. He will not allow the temptation to be more than you can stand. When you are tempted, he will show you a way out so that you can endure. ¹⁴ So, my dear friends, flee from the worship of idols.

DAY THIRTY

Begin the Day by Delighting in an Eternal Attraction
Meditate on and internalize the Apostle Paul's words in I Corinthians 10:

¹² If you think you are standing strong, be careful not to fall. ¹³ The temptations in your life are no different from what others experience. And God is faithful. He will not allow the temptation to be more than you can stand. When you are tempted, he will show you a way out so that you can endure. ¹⁴ So, my dear friends, flee from the worship of idols.

During the Day – Denial of a Modern Attachment
DAY 30: BREAKAWAY DAY

Today's challenge is to make a clean break from all social media! Today's challenge asks for a huge leap – the whole day!! That's right, let's begin our last ten days in a strong fashion with a twenty-four hour BREAKAWAY DAY!!

End the Day by Delighting in an Eternal Attraction
Meditate on and internalize the Apostle Paul's words in I Corinthians 10:

¹² If you think you are standing strong, be careful not to fall. ¹³ The temptations in your life are no different from what others experience. And God is faithful. He will not allow the temptation to be more than you can stand. When you are tempted, he will show you a way out so that you can endure. ¹⁴ So, my dear friends, flee from the worship of idols.

DAY THIRTY ONE

Begin the Day by Delighting in an Eternal Attraction
Meditate on and internalize Ephesians 2: *But God is so rich in mercy, and he loved us so much, 5 that even though we were dead because of our sins, he gave us life when he raised Christ from the dead. (It is only by God's grace that you have been saved!) 6 For he raised us from the dead along with Christ and seated us with him in the heavenly realms because we are united with Christ Jesus. 7 So God can point to us in all future ages as examples of the incredible wealth of his grace and kindness toward us, as shown in all he has done for us who are united with Christ Jesus. 8 God saved you by his grace when you believed. And you can't take credit for this; it is a gift from God. 9 Salvation is not a reward for the good things we have done, so none of us can boast about it. 10 For we are God's masterpiece. He has created us anew in Christ Jesus, so we can do the good things he planned for us long ago.*

During the Day – Denial of a Modern Attachment
DAY 31: SCREENS DOWN

For today's challenge we are going to begin our day and then end our day with screens off for ninety minutes. This means smart phones, televisions, computers, etc. Spend this time – at the beginning and end of the day – focusing on today's delights and just reflect on and prepare for the day ahead.

End the Day by Delighting in an Eternal Attraction
Meditate on and internalize Ephesians 2: *But God is so rich in mercy, and he loved us so much, 5 that even though we were dead because of our sins, he gave us life when he raised Christ from the dead. (It is only by God's grace that you have been saved!) 6 For he raised us from the dead along with Christ and seated us with him in the heavenly realms because we are united with Christ Jesus. 7 So God can point to us in all future ages as examples of the incredible wealth of his grace and kindness toward us, as shown in all he has done for us who are united with Christ Jesus. 8 God saved you by his grace when you believed. And you can't take credit for this; it is a gift from God. 9 Salvation is not a reward for the good things we have done, so none of us can boast about it. 10 For we are God's masterpiece. He has created us anew in Christ Jesus, so we can do the good things he planned for us long ago.*

DAY THIRTY TWO

Begin the Day by Delighting in an Eternal Attraction

Meditate on and internalize Ephesians 2: *But God is so rich in mercy, and he loved us so much, 5 that even though we were dead because of our sins, he gave us life when he raised Christ from the dead. (It is only by God's grace that you have been saved!) 6 For he raised us from the dead along with Christ and seated us with him in the heavenly realms because we are united with Christ Jesus. 7 So God can point to us in all future ages as examples of the incredible wealth of his grace and kindness toward us, as shown in all he has done for us who are united with Christ Jesus. 8 God saved you by his grace when you believed. And you can't take credit for this; it is a gift from God. 9 Salvation is not a reward for the good things we have done, so none of us can boast about it. 10 For we are God's masterpiece. He has created us anew in Christ Jesus, so we can do the good things he planned for us long ago.*

During the Day – Denial of a Modern Attachment
DAY 32: SOCIAL MEDIA DETOX DAY

For today's challenge we are going to disable our notifications and go four hours without viewing, responding to, or checking in with our social media apps. All of the apps you lean on should be included in this six-hour-challenge window.

End the Day by Delighting in an Eternal Attraction

Meditate on and internalize Ephesians 2: *But God is so rich in mercy, and he loved us so much, 5 that even though we were dead because of our sins, he gave us life when he raised Christ from the dead. (It is only by God's grace that you have been saved!) 6 For he raised us from the dead along with Christ and seated us with him in the heavenly realms because we are united with Christ Jesus. 7 So God can point to us in all future ages as examples of the incredible wealth of his grace and kindness toward us, as shown in all he has done for us who are united with Christ Jesus. 8 God saved you by his grace when you believed. And you can't take credit for this; it is a gift from God. 9 Salvation is not a reward for the good things we have done, so none of us can boast about it. 10 For we are God's masterpiece. He has created us anew in Christ Jesus, so we can do the good things he planned for us long ago.*

DAY THIRTY THREE

Begin the Day by Delighting in an Eternal Attraction

Meditate on and internalize Ephesians 2: *But God is so rich in mercy, and he loved us so much, 5 that even though we were dead because of our sins, he gave us life when he raised Christ from the dead. (It is only by God's grace that you have been saved!) 6 For he raised us from the dead along with Christ and seated us with him in the heavenly realms because we are united with Christ Jesus. 7 So God can point to us in all future ages as examples of the incredible wealth of his grace and kindness toward us, as shown in all he has done for us who are united with Christ Jesus. 8 God saved you by his grace when you believed. And you can't take credit for this; it is a gift from God. 9 Salvation is not a reward for the good things we have done, so none of us can boast about it. 10 For we are God's masterpiece. He has created us anew in Christ Jesus, so we can do the good things he planned for us long ago.*

During the Day – Denial of a Modern Attachment
DAY 33: ONE SCREEN AT A TIME

Today's challenge will raise awareness regarding how often we have more than one screen open or active at a time. The *multiple-screen realty*, we've grown accustomed to has created less focused and more highly distracted individuals and culture. Such cultural and personal realities contribute toward us being victimized by the easy diversion porn offers. So, today it's 'one screen at a time' day. This means that when your computer is on, your phone needs to be off. Or, if you are watching a movie, your computer should be turned off and your phone should be inaccessible.

End the Day by Delighting in an Eternal Attraction

Meditate on and internalize Ephesians 2: *But God is so rich in mercy, and he loved us so much, 5 that even though we were dead because of our sins, he gave us life when he raised Christ from the dead. (It is only by God's grace that you have been saved!) 6 For he raised us from the dead along with Christ and seated us with him in the heavenly realms because we are united with Christ Jesus. 7 So God can point to us in all future ages as examples of the incredible wealth of his grace and kindness toward us, as shown in all he has done for us who are united with Christ Jesus. 8 God saved you by his grace when you believed. And you can't take credit for this; it is a gift from God. 9 Salvation is not a reward for the good things we have done, so none of us can boast about it. 10 For we are God's masterpiece. He has created us anew in Christ Jesus, so we can do the good things he planned for us long ago.*

DAY THIRTY FOUR

Begin the Day by Delighting in an Eternal Attraction

Meditate on and internalize Ephesians 2: *But God is so rich in mercy, and he loved us so much, 5 that even though we were dead because of our sins, he gave us life when he raised Christ from the dead. (It is only by God's grace that you have been saved!) 6 For he raised us from the dead along with Christ and seated us with him in the heavenly realms because we are united with Christ Jesus. 7 So God can point to us in all future ages as examples of the incredible wealth of his grace and kindness toward us, as shown in all he has done for us who are united with Christ Jesus. 8 God saved you by his grace when you believed. And you can't take credit for this; it is a gift from God. 9 Salvation is not a reward for the good things we have done, so none of us can boast about it. 10 For we are God's masterpiece. He has created us anew in Christ Jesus, so we can do the good things he planned for us long ago.*

During the Day – Denial of a Modern Attachment
DAY 34: GAMING FREE ZONES

We spend too much time online these days. Some stats indicate that teens spend about nine hours a day on social media apps. The bulk of that time is spent on gaming. Today's challenge is to spend the hours you'd normally be spending gaming on some other activity. You may even try something outdoors!

End the Day by Delighting in an Eternal Attraction

Meditate on and internalize Ephesians 2: *But God is so rich in mercy, and he loved us so much, 5 that even though we were dead because of our sins, he gave us life when he raised Christ from the dead. (It is only by God's grace that you have been saved!) 6 For he raised us from the dead along with Christ and seated us with him in the heavenly realms because we are united with Christ Jesus. 7 So God can point to us in all future ages as examples of the incredible wealth of his grace and kindness toward us, as shown in all he has done for us who are united with Christ Jesus. 8 God saved you by his grace when you believed. And you can't take credit for this; it is a gift from God. 9 Salvation is not a reward for the good things we have done, so none of us can boast about it. 10 For we are God's masterpiece. He has created us anew in Christ Jesus, so we can do the good things he planned for us long ago.*

DAY THIRTY FIVE

Begin the Day by Delighting in an Eternal Attraction

Meditate on and internalize Ephesians 2: *But God is so rich in mercy, and he loved us so much, 5 that even though we were dead because of our sins, he gave us life when he raised Christ from the dead. (It is only by God's grace that you have been saved!) 6 For he raised us from the dead along with Christ and seated us with him in the heavenly realms because we are united with Christ Jesus. 7 So God can point to us in all future ages as examples of the incredible wealth of his grace and kindness toward us, as shown in all he has done for us who are united with Christ Jesus. 8 God saved you by his grace when you believed. And you can't take credit for this; it is a gift from God. 9 Salvation is not a reward for the good things we have done, so none of us can boast about it. 10 For we are God's masterpiece. He has created us anew in Christ Jesus, so we can do the good things he planned for us long ago.*

During the Day – Denial of a Modern Attachment
DAY 35: UNDERSTAND PORN'S POWER AND PERVASIVENESS

Today's challenge invites us to understand, on a deeper level, how pervasive porn has become. My suggestion is that you read an article or two that identifies how porn changes the structure of our brains and how porn is gradually shaping the infrastructure of our culture. I am going to provide some links to websites that will help:
http://fightthenewdrug.org/get-the-facts-2/
http://www.covenanteyes.com/e-books/

End the Day by Delighting in an Eternal Attraction

Meditate on and internalize Ephesians 2: *But God is so rich in mercy, and he loved us so much, 5 that even though we were dead because of our sins, he gave us life when he raised Christ from the dead. (It is only by God's grace that you have been saved!) 6 For he raised us from the dead along with Christ and seated us with him in the heavenly realms because we are united with Christ Jesus. 7 So God can point to us in all future ages as examples of the incredible wealth of his grace and kindness toward us, as shown in all he has done for us who are united with Christ Jesus. 8 God saved you by his grace when you believed. And you can't take credit for this; it is a gift from God. 9 Salvation is not a reward for the good things we have done, so none of us can boast about it. 10 For we are God's masterpiece. He has created us anew in Christ Jesus, so we can do the good things he planned for us long ago.*

DAY THIRTY SIX
Begin the Day by Delighting in an Eternal Attraction

Meditate on and internalize Ephesians 2: *But God is so rich in mercy, and he loved us so much, 5 that even though we were dead because of our sins, he gave us life when he raised Christ from the dead. (It is only by God's grace that you have been saved!) 6 For he raised us from the dead along with Christ and seated us with him in the heavenly realms because we are united with Christ Jesus. 7 So God can point to us in all future ages as examples of the incredible wealth of his grace and kindness toward us, as shown in all he has done for us who are united with Christ Jesus. 8 God saved you by his grace when you believed. And you can't take credit for this; it is a gift from God. 9 Salvation is not a reward for the good things we have done, so none of us can boast about it. 10 For we are God's masterpiece. He has created us anew in Christ Jesus, so we can do the good things he planned for us long ago.*

During the Day – Denial of a Modern Attachment
DAY 36: POSITIVE INPUT ONLY

Today's challenge invites us to 'turn off' any input that is negative and demeaning. Many of us listen to song lyrics that demean others. We often involve ourselves in conversations that tear others down. We love the social media sites that are hyper-critical and mean-spirited. We watch movies, television programs, etc., that accentuate and exploit the worst parts of humanity. For one day we are going to say 'no' to all such input.

End the Day by Delighting in an Eternal Attraction

Meditate on and internalize Ephesians 2: *But God is so rich in mercy, and he loved us so much, 5 that even though we were dead because of our sins, he gave us life when he raised Christ from the dead. (It is only by God's grace that you have been saved!) 6 For he raised us from the dead along with Christ and seated us with him in the heavenly realms because we are united with Christ Jesus. 7 So God can point to us in all future ages as examples of the incredible wealth of his grace and kindness toward us, as shown in all he has done for us who are united with Christ Jesus. 8 God saved you by his grace when you believed. And you can't take credit for this; it is a gift from God. 9 Salvation is not a reward for the good things we have done, so none of us can boast about it. 10 For we are God's masterpiece. He has created us anew in Christ Jesus, so we can do the good things he planned for us long ago.*

DAY THIRTY SEVEN
Begin the Day by Delighting in an Eternal Attraction

Meditate on and internalize Ephesians 2: *But God is so rich in mercy, and he loved us so much, 5 that even though we were dead because of our sins, he gave us life when he raised Christ from the dead. (It is only by God's grace that you have been saved!) 6 For he raised us from the dead along with Christ and seated us with him in the heavenly realms because we are united with Christ Jesus. 7 So God can point to us in all future ages as examples of the incredible wealth of his grace and kindness toward us, as shown in all he has done for us who are united with Christ Jesus. 8 God saved you by his grace when you believed. And you can't take credit for this; it is a gift from God. 9 Salvation is not a reward for the good things we have done, so none of us can boast about it. 10 For we are God's masterpiece. He has created us anew in Christ Jesus, so we can do the good things he planned for us long ago.*

During the Day – Denial of a Modern Attachment
DAY 37: SCREENS DOWN

For today's challenge we are going to begin our day and then end our day with screens off for ninety minutes. This means smart phones, televisions, computers, etc. Spend this time – at the beginning and end of the day – focusing on today's delight and just reflecting on and preparing for the day ahead.

End the Day by Delighting in an Eternal Attraction

Meditate on and internalize Ephesians 2: *But God is so rich in mercy, and he loved us so much, 5 that even though we were dead because of our sins, he gave us life when he raised Christ from the dead. (It is only by God's grace that you have been saved!) 6 For he raised us from the dead along with Christ and seated us with him in the heavenly realms because we are united with Christ Jesus. 7 So God can point to us in all future ages as examples of the incredible wealth of his grace and kindness toward us, as shown in all he has done for us who are united with Christ Jesus. 8 God saved you by his grace when you believed. And you can't take credit for this; it is a gift from God. 9 Salvation is not a reward for the good things we have done, so none of us can boast about it. 10 For we are God's masterpiece. He has created us anew in Christ Jesus, so we can do the good things he planned for us long ago.*

DAY THIRTY EIGHT

Begin the Day by Delighting in an Eternal Attraction

Meditate on and internalize Ephesians 2: *But God is so rich in mercy, and he loved us so much, 5 that even though we were dead because of our sins, he gave us life when he raised Christ from the dead. (It is only by God's grace that you have been saved!) 6 For he raised us from the dead along with Christ and seated us with him in the heavenly realms because we are united with Christ Jesus. 7 So God can point to us in all future ages as examples of the incredible wealth of his grace and kindness toward us, as shown in all he has done for us who are united with Christ Jesus. 8 God saved you by his grace when you believed. And you can't take credit for this; it is a gift from God. 9 Salvation is not a reward for the good things we have done, so none of us can boast about it. 10 For we are God's masterpiece. He has created us anew in Christ Jesus, so we can do the good things he planned for us long ago.*

During the Day – Denial of a Modern Attachment
DAY 38: PRACTICING GRATITUDE THROUGHOUT THE DAY

Today's challenge invites us to go through our day with a particular focus on being grateful for what we have and where we are in life. Shifting our focus toward gratitude might give us greater clarity on our addictions and struggles. Specifically, take a few minutes and jot down three – five reasons you have to be thankful. Carry those reasons with you throughout your day. Porn leverages ingratitude and tricks us to click on what it offers to ease the pain.

End the Day by Delighting in an Eternal Attraction

Meditate on and internalize Ephesians 2: *But God is so rich in mercy, and he loved us so much, 5 that even though we were dead because of our sins, he gave us life when he raised Christ from the dead. (It is only by God's grace that you have been saved!) 6 For he raised us from the dead along with Christ and seated us with him in the heavenly realms because we are united with Christ Jesus. 7 So God can point to us in all future ages as examples of the incredible wealth of his grace and kindness toward us, as shown in all he has done for us who are united with Christ Jesus. 8 God saved you by his grace when you believed. And you can't take credit for this; it is a gift from God. 9 Salvation is not a reward for the good things we have done, so none of us can boast about it. 10 For we are God's masterpiece. He has created us anew in Christ Jesus, so we can do the good things he planned for us long ago.*

DAY THIRTY NINE

Begin the Day by Delighting in an Eternal Attraction

Meditate on and internalize Ephesians 2: *But God is so rich in mercy, and he loved us so much, 5 that even though we were dead because of our sins, he gave us life when he raised Christ from the dead. (It is only by God's grace that you have been saved!) 6 For he raised us from the dead along with Christ and seated us with him in the heavenly realms because we are united with Christ Jesus. 7 So God can point to us in all future ages as examples of the incredible wealth of his grace and kindness toward us, as shown in all he has done for us who are united with Christ Jesus. 8 God saved you by his grace when you believed. And you can't take credit for this; it is a gift from God. 9 Salvation is not a reward for the good things we have done, so none of us can boast about it. 10 For we are God's masterpiece. He has created us anew in Christ Jesus, so we can do the good things he planned for us long ago.*

During the Day – Denial of a Modern Attachment
DAY 39: ACCOUNTABILITY AND ACTION STEPS

Today's challenge invites us to take strategic steps toward accountability and action. One line of accountability is to install blocking/filtering software on your devices. Another might be confessing your problem to a friend or trusted loved one. **Just put one accountability step in place**. Next, take some time and develop three action steps you are going to take that will help protect you against porn's power. These steps are designed to serve as a road map for your journey after this ten-day challenge is over.

End the Day by Delighting in an Eternal Attraction

Meditate on and internalize Ephesians 2: *But God is so rich in mercy, and he loved us so much, 5 that even though we were dead because of our sins, he gave us life when he raised Christ from the dead. (It is only by God's grace that you have been saved!) 6 For he raised us from the dead along with Christ and seated us with him in the heavenly realms because we are united with Christ Jesus. 7 So God can point to us in all future ages as examples of the incredible wealth of his grace and kindness toward us, as shown in all he has done for us who are united with Christ Jesus. 8 God saved you by his grace when you believed. And you can't take credit for this; it is a gift from God. 9 Salvation is not a reward for the good things we have done, so none of us can boast about it. 10 For we are God's masterpiece. He has created us anew in Christ Jesus, so we can do the good things he planned for us long ago.*

DAY FORTY

Begin the Day by Delighting in an Eternal Attraction

Meditate on and internalize Ephesians 2: *But God is so rich in mercy, and he loved us so much, 5 that even though we were dead because of our sins, he gave us life when he raised Christ from the dead. (It is only by God's grace that you have been saved!) 6 For he raised us from the dead along with Christ and seated us with him in the heavenly realms because we are united with Christ Jesus. 7 So God can point to us in all future ages as examples of the incredible wealth of his grace and kindness toward us, as shown in all he has done for us who are united with Christ Jesus. 8 God saved you by his grace when you believed. And you can't take credit for this; it is a gift from God. 9 Salvation is not a reward for the good things we have done, so none of us can boast about it. 10 For we are God's masterpiece. He has created us anew in Christ Jesus, so we can do the good things he planned for us long ago.*

During the Day – Denial of a Modern Attachment
DAY 40: BREAKAWAY DAY

Today's challenge is to make a clean break from all social media! Today's challenge asks for a huge leap – the whole day!! That's right, let's bring our forty-day challenge to a close in strong fashion with a twenty-four hour BREAKAWAY DAY!!

End the Day by Delighting in an Eternal Attraction

Meditate on and internalize Ephesians 2: *But God is so rich in mercy, and he loved us so much, 5 that even though we were dead because of our sins, he gave us life when he raised Christ from the dead. (It is only by God's grace that you have been saved!) 6 For he raised us from the dead along with Christ and seated us with him in the heavenly realms because we are united with Christ Jesus. 7 So God can point to us in all future ages as examples of the incredible wealth of his grace and kindness toward us, as shown in all he has done for us who are united with Christ Jesus. 8 God saved you by his grace when you believed. And you can't take credit for this; it is a gift from God. 9 Salvation is not a reward for the good things we have done, so none of us can boast about it. 10 For we are God's masterpiece. He has created us anew in Christ Jesus, so we can do the good things he planned for us long ago.*

DAY FORTY ONE
CELEBRATE THE PAST TEN DAYS AND COMMIT TO THE NEXT TEN DAYS

Celebrate your successes so that you can accurately reflect on your failures. It's a journey and a long one at that!

NEVER – EVER – GIVE UP HOPE!

Honesty

Self-preservation prevents honesty! If you have acted out, or continue to struggle, it's best to be honest with those whom this impacts the most! Be honest with yourself, the Lord, and your loved ones. This is a difficult place to begin, but if you practice honesty, then you will find that – over time – the deceptive power of porn does decrease.

Openness

Developing a rhythm that is open to scrutiny will help you as you move forward in this walk out of porn. Be sure others have access to your devices. Ask others to hold you accountable, particularly in those areas of known triggers.

Perseverance

Don't give up! I have spoken with countless men who feel like giving in and giving up. Don't swim in that shame. Once you practice honesty and experience openness, then you can assess where you are and reaffirm your desire to be free from porn's pull!

Engagement

Relapse into addiction can lead us into an isolated island of guilt and shame. Don't let that happen. Have an action plan in place that includes re-engaging in meaningful ways with the people you love and those who love you. Engage in a craft, hobby, the community, your church, a special skill or talent. Engaging into the meaningful people and places God has granted will lead you into a life of honesty, openness, perseverance, and engagement.

ABOUT THE AUTHOR

Biz Gainey has been married to Melissa since 1995. They are blessed with three children, now grown. He serves as a pastor of a local church committed to soul-keeping and spiritual formation. He uses accountability software on every electronic device he owns and meets with a group of meet who long for freedom and flourishing in all areas of life. He blogs about spiritual formation, desire, sacred rhythms, and addiction on disruptusenovatus.com.

---

[i] It's been scientifically proven that porn viewing rewires your brain in destructive and dehumanizing ways (http://www.theguardian.com/commentisfree/2013/sep/26/brain-scans-porn-addicts-sexual-tastes or, http://www.fightthenewdrug.org/porn-changes-the-brain/).

[ii] http://www.christianitytoday.com/gleanings/2016/january/how-pastors-struggle-porn-phenomenon-josh-mcdowell-barna.html?utm_source=ctweeklyhtml&utm_medium=Newsletter&utm_term=13033267&utm_content=413064807&utm_campaign=2013

[iii] Smith, James Bryan (2009-12-14). The Good and Beautiful God: Falling in Love with the God Jesus Knows (The Apprentice Series Book 1). InterVarsity Press. Kindle Edition.

[iv] www.exoduscry.com

[v] http://www.digitaltrends.com/movies/the-walking-dead-twitter-favorite-2015/

[vi] http://www.imdb.com/list/ls055027705/

[vii] www.covenanteyes.com/2014/02/03/brain-chemicals-and-porn-addiction/

[viii] Lewis, C. S. Mere Christianity: Comprising The Case for Christianity ; Christian Behaviour and Beyond Personality. New York, NY: Simon & Schuster, 1980. Print.

[ix] Rolheiser, Ronald. Against an Infinite Horizon: The Finger of God in Our Everyday Lives. New York: Crossroad Pub., 2001. Print.

[x] https://www.youtube.com/watch?v=2AH2tJxBmj4

[xi] http://www.covenanteyes.com/pornstats/ and http://www.nbcnews.com/business/business-news/porn-industry-feeling-upbeat-about-2014- n9076)

[xii] http://www.metro.us/news/generation-rapist-is-online-porn-making-boys- violent/tmWmbB---6fKjKZ0XycmIE/

[xiii] http://www.covenanteyes.com/2015/12/29/how-porn-is-keeping-men-from-marriage/?idev_id=997

[xiv] http://www.yourbrainonporn.com/erectile-dysfunction-and-porn
[xv] https://www.washingtonpost.com/news/soloish/wp/2016/06/10/rape-culture-is-a-man-problem-why-arent-more-men-speaking-up/ and http://fightthenewdrug.org/how-porn-is-fueling-sexual-assault-on-college-campuses/
[xvi] https://www.unglobalcompact.org/docs/issues_doc/labour/Forced_labour/HUMAN_TRAFFICKING_-_BACKGROUND_BRIEFING_NOTE_-_final.pdf and http://www.huffingtonpost.com/johnhenry-westen/want-to-stop-sex-traffick_b_6563338.html
[xvii] http://pornharmsresearch.com/2011/04/increases-violence/
[xviii] www.firstthings.com
[xix] http://www.apa.org/news/press/releases/stress/2012/impact.aspx
[xx] Homer; Pope, Alexander (2012-05-16). The Odyssey (p. 208). . Kindle Edition.
[xxi] http://3m37tq2euojp3d9gpf4dbqph.wpengine.netdna-cdn.com/wp-content/uploads/Impact-of-Exposure-to-Sexually-Explicit-and-Exploitative-Materials.pdf
[xxii] http://www.covenanteyes.com/services/internet-accountability/
[xxiii] http://fightthenewdrug.org/the-percentage-of-12-year-olds-who-admit-being-addicted-to-porn-will-shock-you/?utm_content=27589635&utm_medium=social&utm_source=facebook
[xxiv] http://pornharmskids.org.au/
[xxv] http://www.transformingcenter.org/2013/08/part-4-leading-in-rhythm-the-examen-of-consciousness-and-conscience/
[xxvi] Discerning God's Will Together: A Spiritual Practice for the Church by Danny E. Morris
[xxvii] https://www.youtube.com/watch?v=9eEyTw4wylk
[xxviii] Rebecca Konyndyk DeYoung, *New Life in the Desert: Monastic Wisdom for Public Life*: Comment Magazine, 1.16.2014
[xxix] http://www.covenanteyes.com/e-books/
[xxx] http://x3groups.com/

www.ingramcontent.com/pod-product-compliance
Lightning Source LLC
LaVergne TN
LVHW041222080426
835508LV00011B/1039